Praise for
SIMPLE PLEASURES

"*Simple Pleasures* is more than just a cookbook; it is an endearing collection and connection to food as it should be, memorable home cooked dishes made with everyday, quality ingredients that are simply cooked to bring out real, honest-to-goodness flavor with minimal effort."

~ **Mary Ann Esposito,** host of PBS's "Ciao Italia" and author of *Ciao Italia Family Classics*

"Chris and I have cooked many recipes together, but we really bonded behind the stove when we shared our family food stories and our grandmothers' recipes. Congratulations, Chris! You have put all of those wonderful and deliciously simple recipes in a must-have cookbook, along with the added flavors of Daniel Agüera. *Simple Pleasures* is a collection of simple, delicious recipes and memories."

~ **Lidia Bastianich,** host of PBS's "Lidia's Kitchen," restaurateur, author of *Lidia's Mastering the Art of Italian Cuisine* and other books on Italian food traditions

"This is a cookbook for you and me – accessible food, with recipes that you don't have to go to chef school to be able to prepare in your own home. The promise of pleasure comes from big flavors of dishes passed down from the authors' Italian and Spanish grandmothers."

~ **Janet Mendel,** author of *Traditional Spanish Cooking* and other books on the cuisine of Spain

"*Simple Pleasures* focuses on real ingredients, with meals that are simple to prepare and satisfying flavors – exactly what today's cook looks for and needs in his or her kitchen. Chris Fennimore and Daniel Agüera make preparing meals fun again, with engaging stories and recipes for comfort food even the pickiest eaters will enjoy."

~ **Gretchen McKay,** *Pittsburgh Post-Gazette* feature writer/food writer

"I knew I would love the recipes in this cookbook! *Simple Pleasures* is all about a style of cooking that is simple, uncomplicated and respects the use of good ingredients."

~ **Daniel Mancini,** Founder, Mama Mancini's Company

SIMPLE PLEASURES

SIMPLE PLEASURES

RECIPES AND MEMORIES OF REAL FOOD

CHRIS FENNIMORE | DANIEL AGÜERA

Pittsburgh

Simple Pleasures

Recipes and Memories of Real Food

ISBN-13: 978-1-943366-32-3

Library of Congress Control Number: 2017944224
CIP information available upon request

First Edition, 2017

St. Lynn's Press . POB 18680 . Pittsburgh, PA 15236
412.381.9933 . www.stlynnspress.com

Design Conception – Melissa Neely
Layout – Holly Rosborough
Editor – Catherine Dees

Printed in Canada
On certified FSC recycled paper using soy-based inks

This title and all of St. Lynn's Press books may be purchased for educational, business or sales promotional use. For information please write:
Special Markets Department . St. Lynn's Press . POB 18680 . Pittsburgh, PA 15236

10 9 8 7 6 5 4 3 2 1

TO OUR WONDERFUL GRANDMOTHERS,

WHO FIRST TAUGHT US THE SIMPLE PLEASURES

OF COOKING FROM THE HEART

Table of Contents

Introduction

This is a cookbook of simple recipes with simple ingredients that bring back the Simple Pleasures of eating. It is written by two food lovers, one a home cook, the other a chef – both with a deeply held belief in "real food."

CHRIS

Do you ever feel that food has gotten too complicated and recipes too intimidating for everyday cooks? Most of the food we remember so fondly from our childhoods probably did not include bonito flakes or emulsified thistle fronds. Nowadays, our main exposure to cooking is not so much around the kitchen table but in the over-hyped kitchen battlegrounds of cable TV chef competitions. For these culinary combatants no ingredient is too obscure and no technique too tedious. Each dish is plated with a staggering list of ingredients and toppings in architectural and artistic balance. And reading a restaurant menu has become a challenge. There are no more "Shrimp"; they have become "Panamanian Prawns." A deconstructed chicken pot pie might arrive at the table in three separate dishes.

All of this culinary wizardry is fun and has made dining out much more of an adventure than it has ever been. But it has distracted us from the kind of eating that we used to enjoy on a daily basis – full of distinct and satisfying flavors, comforting textures and food memories that stretch back generations.

Chef Daniel Agüera sparked the idea for this book when he posted a recipe on social media of a simple meal of tomato sauce over rice topped with a fried egg – arroz con huevos, a traditional basic dish from his childhood in northern Spain.

I began to think of similar dishes from my own youth, like pastina in chicken broth, fried peppers with egg and potato, rice pudding with big juicy raisins, Davy Crockett toast smothered in confectioner's sugar, eggs poached in pasta with peas. The richness in these dishes doesn't come from expensive ingredients or the complexity of their preparation, but rather from the warmth of the memories they evoke of simpler times.

Chef Daniel and I were blessed to have had loving grandmothers who taught us about food from the time we could walk – immersing us in flavors and textures that somehow became part of what we knew as love. His Spanish *abuela* showed him how to cook from the heart, trusting his senses and skills. My Southern Italian "Gram" performed small miracles in her tiny Brooklyn kitchen every day. On Sundays, my sisters and I would climb up on chairs at her kitchen table to trim green beans, shape meatballs or mix chopped parsley into the ricotta. Again, the simple pleasures.

Buon appetito!

DANIEL

During the final phase of my culinary education in Spain, the first assignment was to interpret a classic dish, to take a standard recipe and make it our own. Until this point, we were expected to do as we were told. But now we were asked to approach our work not only as craftsmen, but as creators. The purpose of this exercise was to help us begin to develop and strengthen our own unique viewpoint and master the ability to express this vision on a plate.

I completed that assignment a long time ago but think of it often, especially when I try a dish that is offered as a "fresh take" or "new twist" on a classic recipe. Sometimes the remix is delightful; often it is just puzzling, making me wonder whether the person responsible for a particular interpretation is really familiar with the original version. In those cases, the chef might have been better off simply creating something new.

But I'm no purist. I'm as intrigued by new ingredients, preparations, techniques and flavors as any chef. Experimenting in the kitchen is a chef's chance to play. That's important. Equally important is the way that making and eating food creates connections among people – individuals and generations, staff and customers, families and communities. Maybe you'll create an edible work of art using a palette of flavor, texture, scent and color. Or maybe you'll make a sandwich. The point is, very simply, to cook for one another.

Buen provecho!

* * *

Our book brings together recipes from our families' best-loved comfort food traditions, and from American comfort food classics that should always have a place at the table. In all cases, the ingredients are accessible and the cooking techniques are basic and intuitive.

We encourage you to make these recipes with and for your children so they can develop a palate based on essential flavors and textures. You will be giving them food memories they will carry through life and pass on to their own children.

Enjoy!

SIMPLE TOOLS

There is a modern myth that presumes you need a special tool in order to be successful in the kitchen. Our counters and drawers are cluttered with spiralizers, frothers, choppers, poachers, separators and "magic pots." There is an entire industry devoted to kitchen gadgets.

Chris – *I will confess to my own cluttered collection of peelers, scoops and spatulas and I couldn't get by without my stand mixer, food processor and stick blender. But there are several tools that have stood the test of time and fit well into the concept of simple cooking. Chef Daniel and I have assembled a short list:*

BENCH SCRAPER

Chris – *This rectangular square of metal may get the most use of any utensil in my kitchen's "junk" drawer. I use it to work dough on my wooden kneading board, portion out dough for loaves or rolls – even to rough chop vegetables and herbs and to smash garlic cloves.*

CAST IRON SKILLETS

How do we love them? Let us count the ways: Inexpensive, indestructible, best pans for heat retention and distribution, non-stick and impervious to metal utensils.

CHINA CAP

The mesh is so fine on the china cap that you can use it in place of cheesecloth to strain the moisture from homemade cheese. It also gives a beautiful clear broth when you use it to strain your chicken stock. Think strainer on steroids.

FOLEY FOOD MILL

The genius of the food mill lies in its ability to simultaneously puree cooked foods and vegetables and to separate skins, seeds and stems from the finished product.

Chris – *It's my favorite for Sunday Sauce and Applesauce.*

MICROPLANE

Say goodbye to the scraped knuckles from grating cheese on a box grater. Based on the woodworker's rasp, microplanes come in a wide variety of sizes for everything from shredding mozzarella to finely grating nutmeg.

MORTAR AND PESTLE

With the advent of home food processors, it may seem as though the need for this primitive looking kitchen device has diminished. But there is something satisfying about grinding your own spices to the exact texture and consistency you like for your recipes.

Daniel – *At home, my grandmother had a small wooden mortar and pestle with garlic and sea salt in it at all times. A little smash, a little rub, and the freshest garlic salt was ready.*

The mortar and pestle is so universal in Spanish kitchens that its absence in U.S. kitchens surprised me. Here and there, you'll find cooks like Chris or my friend Marla who keep a mortar and pestle handy. You should try using them, too. Nothing extracts the oils and flavors of herbs and citrus like a good smashing with the pestle! That fresh aroma takes over your kitchen and leads you on the journey to a great dish.

PARCHMENT PAPER

This simple tool makes us feel like wizards in the kitchen when the stickiest of cookies literally slide off the parchment. It's also useful for a variety of other kitchen uses like making little pouches to cook fish and vegetables.

RICER

There is no other way to achieve light and fluffy mashed potatoes. It is also the perfect tool for extracting moisture from cooked spinach, grated potatoes, etc.

THERMOMETER

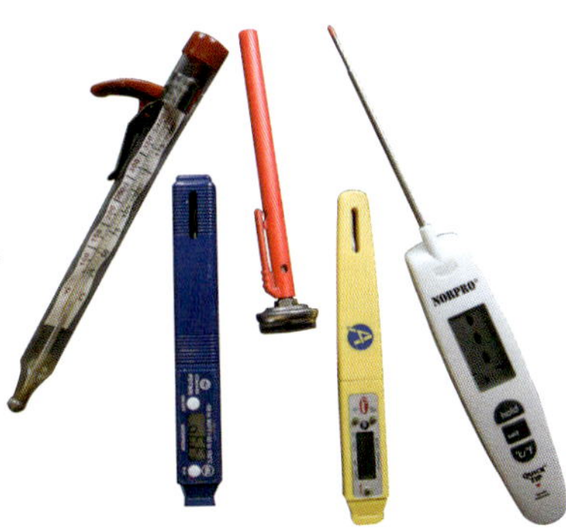

Why guess when you can know exactly when your food is done, or safe? Instant-read thermometers now register temperatures all the way from freezing to boiling sugar for candy making.

WOODEN SPOONS

Aside from being things of beauty that connect us with all our cooking ancestors, wooden spoons are usually the best tool for the job – mixing, stirring, folding. And the handles don't get hot when you leave the spoon in the pot.

Daniel – *For various reasons, wooden spoons aren't often used in restaurants anymore. Before they were banned, a wooden spoon was like a maestro's conducting baton in the hands of a chef, including my grandmother. Chefs would use them to point, gesture for emphasis, or even threaten. My grandmother delivered a few well-deserved smacks with a wooden spoon. The memories of her shaking that spoon in the air will forever be dear to me. From time to time, I see a nice piece of wood and think, "That would make a good wooden spoon." I have quite a stash of these pieces of wood by now. One of these days when I have plenty of spare time I may carve some spoons again as I did when I was a kid.*

TEMPERATURE CONVERSION CHART

The cooking temperatures given in the book are shown in Fahrenheit (°F). For our readers using metric, here are the Celsius (°C) equivalents for the temperatures you'll encounter:

FAHRENHEIT	CELSIUS
115	46.1
160	71.1
165	74
200	93.3
275	135
300	148.9
350	176.7
365	185
375	190.5
400	204.4
425	218.3
450	232.2
475	246.1

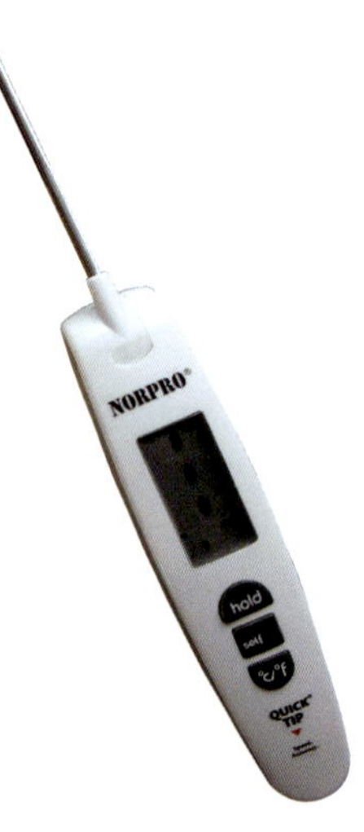

RECIPES

BREAD AND SUCH

Chris – Like the song says, let's start at the very beginning. Making bread is a miracle that transforms lifeless flour and pure water into one of the simplest and most satisfying of pleasures. It is both a miracle to create and a delight to consume and so it has been for millennia.

Every culture has its variations. One of my great childhood pleasures was to dip a plain piece of bread into the Sunday tomato sauce as it simmered on the stove. And the first solid food of any baby in our family is a hunk of bread for them to gnaw on.

Daniel – The smell of bread rising and bread baking can trigger early childhood memories of home. In my mind, I can still see the corner of the kitchen table right against the wall where the bread would rise, covered with a kitchen towel. I remember peeking under those towels many times, wondering what was going on under there.

Chris

These two recipes really belong together because they create one of the most satisfying combinations of simple pleasures – bread and butter. That phrase has crept its way into our vernacular to stand for the very basics, the things we are most comfortable with. But real bread and butter has fallen out of the repertoire of most home cooks. Milk, honey, yeast, flour and a little salt are all that are needed to create this dynamic duo of comfort foods.

A NOTE ABOUT FLOUR

I generally use bread flour or high-gluten flour for this recipe, but all-purpose flour works just fine.

Milk and Honey Bread with Homemade Butter

Makes ½ pound of butter (plus 2 cups of whey or buttermilk) and 2 loaves of bread

BREAD

INGREDIENTS

2 cups whey (you can also use regular milk or buttermilk)

¼ cup warm water (115°F)

2 teaspoons dry yeast

¼ cup honey

5 cups flour

1 teaspoon salt

STEPS

- Dissolve the yeast in the warm water. Add the honey and stir to combine. The yeast should begin to foam.
- Put the flour and the whey into the bowl of a stand mixer. Add the yeast and honey mixture and finally the salt.
- Beat on low speed with the dough hook until the mixture is combined. Increase the speed a notch and continue to knead until the dough forms a ball and cleans the side of the bowl. This should take around 5 minutes. If the dough appears very stiff and dry you can add a few tablespoons of water. If it is too wet you can add a few tablespoons more of flour.
- Take out the dough hook and cover the bowl. Let the dough rise for about an hour. It should double in size.
- Preheat the oven to 350°F.
- Coat the inside of 2 loaf pans with nonstick spray.

BREAD STEPS (continued)

- Sprinkle a little flour on your work surface and pull the dough out of the bowl. Cut it in half. Press one half into an approximate 8-inch square. Roll it up tightly and place, seam side down, into one of the pans. Repeat with the remaining dough. Cover loosely with a towel and let rise again until the dough is an inch or more above the rim of the pan.
- Bake the loaves for 35–40 minutes or until a thermometer registers over 200°F. Let the loaves cool in the pan for 5 minutes and then empty onto a rack to cool completely.
- Cut into thick slices with a serrated knife and enjoy with a big slather of your fresh butter.

BUTTER

INGREDIENTS

1 quart heavy cream (avoid the ultra-pasteurized if possible)

Salt to taste

STEPS

- Add the cream to the bowl of a stand mixer fitted with the paddle attachment. Turn the machine on low. In a few minutes the cream will begin to thicken. A little bit longer and the cream will start to stiffen. And finally, the butter and whey will separate in the bowl.
- Use your hands to gather the butter together and squeeze any excess moisture back into the bowl.
- Place the butter on a flat surface, knead in a little salt, if desired, and shape into a log or press it into a crock.

Davy Crockett Toast

Makes 2 Davy Crocketts

INGREDIENTS

2 thick slices homemade bread

4 pats butter

Powdered sugar

STEPS

- Heat a large skillet over medium heat. Add 2 pats of butter and place the bread slices over the butter, sliding them around to distribute the butter. Add a pat of butter to the top of each slice.
- Cook until browned on the top and flip to brown the second side. Sprinkle liberally with powdered sugar and serve immediately.
- These are best hot out of the pan.

Chris

I tried to research the origin of this name for a dish my mother made for me as a special treat when I was home sick from school or on occasional Saturday mornings. I seem to remember that she always suggested it when she thought I was a little down in the dumps. After a pretty exhaustive online search, I have come to the conclusion that it was just a clever way for Mom to try and cheer me up. I was a big fan of Davy Crockett (there are embarrassing pictures of me in a coonskin cap which we will NOT include here) and the use of his name elevated the status of this simple sweetened toast.

Daniel

Breakfasts of magdalenas and hot chocolate were a big part of growing up, and I still enjoy them as a breakfast or snack. If the name and flavor remind you of French madeleines, it's no accident – this is a Spanish version of that classic treat, but bigger and heartier, a more muffin-like pastry. Try them and you may prefer them to madeleines – and muffins, too.

This recipe is interesting in that it recreates the heating pattern of an old-fashioned brick baking oven, which would be heated to a peak temperature and then lose heat gradually as bakers raked out the coals and filled the oven with bread dough or pastry.

Magdalenas are traditionally made in baking pans lined with paper muffin cups, but you know your bakeware best: if you trust your muffin pan, you can coat the individual muffin wells with nonstick baking spray, butter, or nothing at all as you see fit.

Magdalenas (Olive Oil Muffins)

Makes 12 magdalenas

INGREDIENTS

1 cup sugar, plus more for sprinkling

3 eggs

Zest of ½ lemon

1 cup olive oil

¼ cup milk

1 teaspoon baking powder

¼ teaspoon cinnamon

¼ teaspoon salt

2 cups cake flour

STEPS

- In the bowl of a stand mixer, cream sugar and eggs at medium speed. Continue at medium speed while adding lemon zest, olive oil and milk.
- In a separate mixing bowl, whisk together flour, baking powder, cinnamon and salt. Reduce the speed of the mixer and add the flour mixture. Gradually increase mixer speed to high and whip batter for 3 minutes. Put the mixing bowl in the fridge for 45 minutes.
- Ten or 15 minutes before you're ready to bake, heat the oven to 475°F.
- Prepare the muffin pan using paper baking cups, nonstick baking spray or other preparation. Evenly divide batter among wells in the muffin tin, filling each one ½–¾ full. Sprinkle a little sugar on top of each magdalena.
- Put the muffin pan in the oven, lowering temperature to 350°F. Bake for about 15 minutes, or until a toothpick or cake tester poked into a magdalena comes out dry.
- Enjoy with thick, bittersweet hot chocolate, coffee, juice or milk, according to your age, time of day, or personal preference.

Chris

There is nothing wrong with a nice, gooey, grilled cheese sandwich. But when I was growing up we looked forward to a different kind of cheese sandwich for a Saturday lunch. It was made with ricotta and mozzarella, but the distinctive cheese flavor came from the addition of caciocavallo (which means saddlebags in Italian). The name comes from the way the balls of cheese are tied with string and hung over a rafter or wooden beam to dry and age. It is reminiscent of provolone with a salty and smoky character. You can easily substitute provolone if the more exotic cheese is unavailable.

(In the Sicilian dialect spoken by my Gram, caciocavallo sounded to a child's ear like "ghas gavalda" and it took me many years to track down the real thing.)

SERVING OPTION

You can also put 2 halves together for an even heartier sandwich.

Ricotta and Mozzarella Sandwiches

Makes 8 open-faced sandwiches

INGREDIENTS

4 soft Italian rolls, split

8 ounces whole milk ricotta

8 slices fresh mozzarella

1 cup shredded caciocavallo (or provolone)

Freshly ground black pepper

STEPS

- Spread each half of the rolls with ricotta and season with fresh cracked pepper. Cover with a slice of mozzarella and a handful of the shredded caciocavallo.
- Lay the sandwich halves on a foil-lined baking sheet and broil for just a minute or two, until the cheese is bubbling.

Chris

If you ask for biscuits and jam in England, you'll probably get a plate of flat dry crackers and a small dish of preserves. But around here we like our biscuits fresh from the oven, light and flaky with a golden crust. You can enjoy them as a breakfast bread with eggs and sausage gravy but they might be best of all when split and served with a dollop of fresh jam.

This recipe for freezer jam means you don't need any special canning equipment or expertise, and because the fruit is never cooked it retains its fresh-picked flavors.

This recipe makes a delicious jam with minimum work. It is kept in the freezer because it has not technically been preserved like traditional jams. It will keep in the freezer for months and, once opened, it will easily keep a week in the refrigerator. Freezer jam can be made with any kind of fresh berries or fruit, but strawberries seem to hold up particularly well.

Biscuits and Jam

Makes about 12 biscuits and 5 cups of jam

BISCUITS

INGREDIENTS

2 cups flour

2 teaspoons baking powder

½ teaspoon baking soda

½ teaspoon salt

1 tablespoon sugar

½ cup shortening

¾ cup buttermilk

STEPS

- Preheat the oven to 425°F.
- In a large bowl, mix together the flour, sugar, baking powder, baking soda and salt. Cut in the shortening with a pastry cutter as you would for pie crust until the mixture is crumbly with pea-sized pieces of shortening.
- Pour in the buttermilk all at once and stir gently with a fork, just until the dough clings together in a ball.
- Put the dough on a well floured board and knead ten times, dusting with flour only if necessary. The dough should be springy and elastic.
- Dust the top with a little flour and roll out gently to ½-inch thickness. Use a 2½-inch cutter (or the top of a juice glass) to cut out rounds and place them on a greased cookie sheet with the edges touching. Push the remaining dough together and cut out the rest.
- Bake for 12–15 minutes or until puffed up and golden brown on top.
- Eat them as soon as possible after they come out of the oven!

FREEZER JAM

INGREDIENTS

2 cups ripe, hulled strawberries (about one quart)

4 cups granulated sugar

1 package pectin

¾ cup water

STEPS

- Wash and dry about five 1-cup jelly jars.
- Use a potato masher to make a rough puree of the strawberries. Stir in the sugar and let sit for about 10 minutes.
- Dissolve the packet of pectin in the water and stir over heat while it comes to a boil. Boil for about 1 minute and then add to the strawberries, stirring until most of the sugar is dissolved. There may still be a few granules.
- Pour into the jars, leaving about ½ inch at the top. Wipe the rims and screw on the covers. Let the jelly sit at room temperature for a day. Then it is ready to use or store in the fridge for a week or in the freezer for up to a year!

Welch's grape jelly was our sweet spread of choice. It went on our toast with peanut butter, cream cheese or butter. We spread it on crackers and English muffins. I don't think it was so popular because of any outstanding flavor characteristics. It just came in the cutest glass jars with cartoon characters. Our cupboards were overflowing with these colorful and whimsical little drinking glasses. Something for free! And much quicker and easier than saving Bazooka Bubble Gum wrappers to send in for a prize.

Chris

In my neighborhood in Brooklyn there was a pizzeria on every other corner. A slice was nice but my mother made pizza at home. What I really looked forward to at the pizzerias were zeppoli. They would take little pieces of the pizza dough and drop them into the deep fryer. In just a few seconds they looked like deep brown asteroids from outer space. Three or four of these little fried dough balls were thrown into a paper bag and completely doused with powdered sugar. The bag was closed and shaken until the zeppoli were completely coated.

Zeppoli

Makes about 24 zeppoli

INGREDIENTS

1½ teaspoons yeast

1 teaspoon sugar

1 cup warm water (115°F)

1 tablespoon olive oil

1½ cups flour

Oil for deep frying

Powdered sugar

STEPS

- Sprinkle the yeast and sugar on top of the warm water. Add the olive oil and wait for the yeast to foam.
- Put the flour in a bowl and stir in the yeast mixture. Stir for a few minutes until a stiff batter forms. Sprinkle on a tablespoon or so of additional flour and stir until the batter just starts to clean the side of the bowl. Cover and let rest for one hour. It should double in size.
- In the deep fryer, heat the cooking oil to 365°F and drop in golf-ball-sized pieces of dough. Cook until well browned.
- Drain on paper towels and dredge in powdered sugar.

Chris

My mom made pizza every Friday night of my childhood. She had well-seasoned black square pans that were perfect for our style of thick-crusted Sicilian pizza. She really had it down to a science. Mix the dough at 3:00 pm; put in the pans and top with sauce and cheese at 4:00 pm; into the oven at 5:00 pm; out on the table at 5:30 pm. At the request of my father, Mom always made 5 pizzas. That allowed for plenty at mealtime and at least one pan to enjoy cold the next morning as we all gathered around the television to watch cartoons. This recipe is a little scaled down from Mom's.

Pizza Dough

Makes 2 thick-crust or 3 thin-crust pizzas

INGREDIENTS

2 cups lukewarm water

2 tablespoons olive oil

3 teaspoons yeast (or one package)

1 tablespoon sugar

4 cups high-gluten bread flour, divided

1 tablespoon salt

STEPS

- Heat the water to 120°F. Stir in the olive oil, yeast and sugar and let stand 5–10 minutes while the yeast develops.
- In a bowl, mix the salt with 3 cups of the flour, then stir in the liquid. Stir until well blended and smooth. (You can use the dough hook on your stand mixer, but one of the simple pleasures of this recipe is to get your hands in the warm and supple dough.)
- Once the dough is smooth, add the remaining flour a few tablespoons at a time until the dough is dry enough to turn out on a floured board to knead. Continue to knead and add flour as needed until the dough is no longer very sticky. The less flour you use, the more delicate the dough will be.
- Put the dough in a large greased bowl and cover. Let it sit until it has doubled in size.
- The dough is now ready to be cut and spread into pans or used for any number of pizza dough-based recipes like calzones, breadsticks and focaccia.

A FEW WORDS ABOUT YEAST

People tell me that they have no "luck" with yeast. But the only thing you can do to kill yeast is to dissolve it in water over 130°F. Cooler temperatures won't kill the yeast, only increase the amount of time it takes for the product to rise. Do yourself a favor and get an instant-read thermometer. Test the water temperature before you stir in the yeast. You'll never have a problem with yeast again.

And one more tip: if you are going to be doing any baking, it is much more economical to buy yeast in bulk. A little package containing 2¼ teaspoons can cost as much as $.70 but you can buy a two-pound bag of yeast for around $4.00.

Daniel

I make sourdough bread with my own starter. Starter is a culture of yeast and bacteria that feeds on water and flour, producing the bubbles that make sourdough bread rise and give it its tangy "sourdough" flavor. To maintain a starter, you must add water and flour on a regular basis. Of course the starter grows as you feed it, so whenever you feed it you also have to throw some of it away. It feels wasteful to discard all that bubbly, delicious starter, so ideally you can put it straight into a recipe and bake it. Here is one of my favorites.

Churros are traditionally made with boiling water. Boiling water would kill the yeast in the starter, so use hot tap water instead for this recipe. You can use a fryer if you have one, but the larger surface area of a big sauté pan actually makes it easier to work with the churros.

ABOUT HYDRATION

The recipe calls for sourdough starter at "100% hydration." That means that the starter should be equal parts flour and water, a fairly runny mixture.

Sourdough Churros

Makes about 16 churros

INGREDIENTS

½ cup sourdough starter (100% hydration)

2 cups plus 1 tablespoon all-purpose or high-gluten flour

1½ teaspoons salt

2 cups plus 1 tablespoon hot water (not boiling)

Oil for frying

Granulated sugar or confectioner's sugar for dusting

STEPS

- Mix the sourdough starter, flour and salt. Add the hot water and mix until you get a smooth, runny dough, maybe a little thicker than pancake batter. Let the dough rest for about 20 minutes while you heat the oil.
- Pour 1–1½ inches of oil in a sauté pan and heat to 350°F.
- Pour the dough into a pastry bag with a large tip. (Of course, if you have a churrera – a big dough syringe made especially for churros – use it instead!) Squeeze dough into the hot oil gently but quickly and "cut" the stream of dough with a butter knife when each churro is the desired size. You may fry 3 or 4 churros at a time, or make a spiral of dough in the oil and cut it into pieces later.
- Fry to a golden brown, turning the dough over in the oil to ensure even cooking and color. Remove the churros from the oil when golden brown and put them on a plate lined with paper towels to absorb extra oil.
- Sand them with granulated sugar while they are hot, or (as my daughters prefer) wait until they cool to powder them with confectioner's sugar. They are also delicious with cinnamon sugar or honey.
- Serve with rich, thick hot chocolate.

SOUP'S ON

Chris – I always thought of "soup" as an onomatopoetic word – the sound you make as you slurp a big spoonful of rich broth filled with delicious ingredients that have been slowly simmered into tender goodness. Other than the hottest days of summer, soup was an essential part of our daily diet.

Another great feature of soup is that it is endlessly adaptable to the ingredients at hand and nearly foolproof. And soup is the magician's hat where you can dump in leftover little bits of meat, vegetables, rice and pasta to create one-of-a-kind masterpieces. Your soups may never be the same twice but they are always nourishing and economical.

Daniel – Soup and stew recipes can be good "entry level" recipes. They are usually very forgiving, easily accommodating substitutions, with preparation and assembly at a comfortable pace, and often no advanced techniques are required. If your ingredients are good and you take some reasonable care in preparing them, even novice cooks can produce very tasty results.

Let's start with a basic chicken stock and explore a few variations.

Chris

The key to great soup is great broth. And this simple recipe will provide about 1 gallon of the liquid gold to use or freeze. When I make chicken, I save all the trimmings (breast bones, wing tips, etc.) in a freezer bag. Once the bag is full it's time to make stock. You can even use the chicken or turkey carcass after it has been roasted.

Chicken Broth

Makes 4 quarts

INGREDIENTS

1 chicken or 3 pounds chicken parts

1 onion, skin on

1 stalk celery (with leaves)

1 carrot, washed

1 bay leaf

5 peppercorns

STEPS

- Rinse the chicken and put it in a large stock pot with 5 quarts of water. Add all the other ingredients and bring to a boil. Lower the heat to a simmer and skim any froth that has formed on top of the pot. Simmer, partially covered for 1 hour.
- Remove the chicken to a colander over a bowl and let sit until it is cool enough to handle. Separate the meat from the skin and bones and reserve.
- Return the skin and bones to the pot along with any accumulated drippings and simmer for another 3 hours, until the liquid is reduced to approximately 4 quarts.
- Use a strainer or a China cap (photo at right) to pour the broth into a container. Discard the remaining skin, bones and vegetables.
- Let the broth cool and then refrigerate overnight. A layer of fat will form on the top and the liquid will become gelatinous. Remove the fat. The broth is now ready to be used in a recipe or stored in the freezer in 1-quart zipper bags.

Chris

The best part of having a cold in our house was the regular doses of pastina as a cure-all. It was often served as the first solid food for infants because of its nutritive value and easy digestibility. Pastina is very finely cut pasta in the shape of stars!

Pastina in Brodo

Makes 4 servings

INGREDIENTS

1 tablespoon butter

1 small onion, diced very fine

1 small carrot, diced fine

½ stalk celery, diced fine

½ cup pastina

1 quart chicken broth

STEPS

- Melt the butter over medium heat in a 3-quart saucepan. Add the onion, carrot and celery and sauté gently until they are softened but not brown.
- Add the broth and bring to a boil.
- Stir in the pastina and cook until it is tender, about 5–6 minutes.
- Serve it just as it is or add some of the reserved chicken cut into small pieces and top with grated Romano cheese.

Escarole Soup

Makes 4 servings

INGREDIENTS

1 bunch escarole

2–3 cloves garlic (slapped with the flat of a knife to loosen skin)

3 tablespoons olive oil

2 cups water

STEPS

- Thoroughly clean the escarole to remove any sandy grit. Tear the leaves into smaller pieces.
- Sauté the garlic in the olive oil. As soon as it starts to brown, remove the garlic and add the water. Bring the water to a simmer and add the escarole.
- Cook 5 minutes until the escarole is tender.

Chris

At least three times a week, my grandmother would preface whatever we were having for dinner with a steaming bowl of "zuppa scarola" or escarole soup. She would hold up the ladle and ask everyone "Do you want some scarole?" I had no idea what it was. It just looked green and slimy. Now I wish I had said yes every time. Escarole has a very mild flavor and it is the most tender of all the soup greens. It only needs to cook for a minute or two.

Chris

Lentils are the legumes that put "simple" into the pleasures and satisfying goodness of beans. Since lentils require no overnight soaking or other pre-treatment, they can be ready to enjoy in no time. The longer you cook them the creamier they become.

NOTE

This recipe can be vegan or not, with the option of using either olive oil or a ham hock.

Lentil Soup

Makes 8 servings

INGREDIENTS

1 pound lentils (red, brown, green or mixed)

2 quarts cold water

1 small onion, finely chopped

1 stalk celery, finely chopped

2–3 tablespoons olive oil (or substitute 1 smoked ham hock)

Salt and pepper to taste

½ cup stewed or canned tomatoes (optional)

1 bunch escarole (optional)

STEPS

- Wash lentils and place in a pot with cold water. Chop vegetables and add to lentils. Add olive oil (or ham hock), salt and pepper and tomatoes. Cook over medium heat until the lentils are soft, about 2 hours.
- Clean the escarole well and add 5 minutes before serving.
- If using a ham hock, remove it from the soup and trim off the meat. Chop it into small chunks and add back to the soup.

Chris

The first time I made this dish it was from a recipe in *Bon Appétit* magazine. The results were delicious but the preparation was anything but simple and the use of cream to finish the final soup meant that it was a caloric heavyweight. The advantage of this version is that you have the added sweetness of the caramelized squash and none of the fat and calories from the cream.

Roasted Butternut Squash Soup

Makes 4–6 servings

INGREDIENTS

1 medium butternut squash (should yield about 4 cups)

4 tablespoons butter

1 large onion, diced

½ teaspoon thyme

2 cups water

4 cups chicken stock

STEPS

- Preheat the oven to 350°F.
- Split the squash in half lengthwise and remove the seeds. Place cut side down on a piece of parchment paper in a baking pan and bake for one hour, until the squash is easily pierced with a fork. Allow to cool.
- Melt the butter in a 4-quart soup pot and add the onion, cooking over low heat until nice and brown. This develops a sweet and nutty flavor.
- Add the thyme, water and chicken stock and turn up the heat. Scoop out the flesh of the squash and put it in the pot. Reduce the heat and simmer for one hour.
- Puree the soup with an immersion blender, food processor or blender.
- Serve with a dollop of sour cream and a sprinkling of toasted hazelnuts for an elegant presentation.

Pasta e Fagioli

Makes 6–8 servings

INGREDIENTS

1 onion, chopped

1 carrot, finely diced

1 celery stalk, chopped

2 tablespoons olive oil

2 cloves garlic, mashed

2 cans chickpeas (garbanzos), drained and rinsed

1 quart chicken stock

Salt and pepper to taste

Red pepper flakes (optional)

1 pound ditali or tubetti pasta

Romano cheese

STEPS

- Sauté the onion, carrot and celery in the olive oil until softened. Add the mashed garlic and then the beans. Use the back of a spoon or a potato masher to crush some of the beans.
- Add the chicken stock and bring to a simmer. Season with salt and pepper and the red pepper flakes if you like a little heat.
- Prepare the macaroni according to package directions, but cook it about 2 minutes less than recommended. Drain and reserve some of the pasta liquid.
- Add the macaroni to the beans mixture and allow to cook for another minute so the pasta can absorb some of the stock and the mixture can thicken. Use the reserved pasta water to adjust the consistency to your liking – soupy or thick.
- Serve with freshly grated Romano cheese.

Chris

We called this classic Italian comfort food "pasta fazool." But the real name simply means pasta & beans – a complete meal of starch and protein. What I have come to realize is that there are as many variations of this dish as there are Italian grandmas. We enjoyed a very basic version made with ditali or tubetti macaroni and ceci beans (chickpeas or garbanzo beans). My father often said he would rather have his fill of pasta e fagioli than a fancy piece of steak.

VARIATIONS

You can use other beans such as cannellini, great northern, fava, kidney, pinto, etc. And you can use any of the small pastas like the little shells or ditalini, tubettini, farfalle, etc. But you can also change the flavor profile by adding some tomato sauce or simply adding some fresh tomatoes when you are sautéing the vegetables.

Daniel

If you want to be really authentic with this recipe, you'll make it on October 19. Tradition says that on that date in 1836, the people of Oviedo disarmed an entire battalion of opponents by welcoming them into town with a great afternoon feast of this soup, along with other heavy dishes and plenty of wine. That's why this soup is called "desarme" (disarmament) in Spanish. It is best consumed as those long-ago soldiers enjoyed it: well away from firearms, with a glass of wine or cider, followed by a refreshing nap.

Don't feel too constrained by the October 19th legend: desarme is also often served during Lent because it contains no meat.

Salted Cod and Garbanzo Bean Soup

Makes 8 servings

INGREDIENTS

1 pound dry garbanzo beans (chickpeas)

1 pound salted cod

3 tablespoons olive oil (and a little more), divided

2 bay leaves

2 eggs

1 slice bread (preferably from a few-days-old baguette)

3 cloves garlic

½ cup parsley

1 onion, small diced

1 tablespoon spanish smoked paprika (pimentón)

1 pound frozen spinach

STEPS

- Soak the garbanzo beans in plenty of cold water overnight.
- Follow the salted cod directions for soaking and preparation. Some salted cod might require an overnight process.
- Drain and rinse the beans, then cover them with warm water in a large cooking pot. The beans should be below the surface of the water by at least 1½ inches. Pour 1 tablespoon of olive oil into the water, add the bay leaves, and set over high heat.
- Hard boil the eggs: in a small saucepan, cover eggs with cold water and bring to a boil over medium heat. Immediately remove the saucepan from heat. Cover with a lid and set aside for no longer than ten minutes. Now cover the eggs with cold or even ice water to stop them from becoming overcooked. Set the eggs aside in their cold water to cool.
- In a sauté pan add 2 tablespoons of the olive oil. Fry the bread on both sides. Remove from pan and put in a food processor. Lightly toast the garlic cloves, making sure they don't burn, and add to the bread. Add the parsley.

- When the beans begin to boil, reduce to medium heat. Skim any white foam from the surface of the pot and discard.
- Add a little extra oil to the pan you cooked the bread and garlic in, and sauté the onion. Add the pimentón to the onion and mix in for a few minutes. Add the onion mixture to the garbanzo pot.
- Remove the egg yolks from the eggs and add the yolks to the food processor. Add half a cup of the garbanzo stock and blend until you have a creamy paste.
- Once the garbanzo beans are tender, incorporate the cod into the mixture by tearing small pieces with your fingers. Stir in the bread and egg yolk paste from the processor and bring to a boil. Reduce to a simmer and add the spinach. Allow it to cook for at least 10 more minutes for all flavors to come together.

NOTES

Preparation for this recipe must begin the night before, by soaking the garbanzo beans and perhaps the salt cod, depending on how it has been preserved. Follow the salted cod directions for soaking and preparation.

I don't recommend canned garbanzo beans for this recipe. The stock made from canned beans is not as good.

Daniel

I first met Chris Fennimore when he came to check out "Fat Club." Fat Club was a gathering of chefs and kitchen folk we once held monthly. The theme of that particular month's gathering was fall/harvest ingredients. I concocted a soup out of the harvest flavors that were inspiring me at the time and strangely enough the recipe turned out to be vegan – meaning that it contained only plant-based ingredients (although a ham bone would have been great in that vegetable stock, too).

Chris loved the soup and invited me to make it on a soup-themed show he was scheduled to film. We cooked this soup together in front of the cameras, and we have been friends ever since. This soup might have more ingredients than any of the other dishes in this book, but they are simple ingredients in a simple preparation that almost everybody can enjoy together.

Harvest Soup

Makes 8 servings

INGREDIENTS

1 cup dried garbanzo beans (soaked overnight)

2 tablespoons extra virgin olive oil

3 large garlic cloves, minced

10–12 Marcona almonds (regular blanched almonds will work as well)

1 Spanish onion, diced small

1 teaspoon pimentón (smoked paprika)

2 tablespoons tomato paste

10 cups vegetable stock

1 carrot, diced in 1-inch pieces

1 tablespoon red wine vinegar

1 pinch saffron

1 pound pumpkin or butternut squash, cut into 1-inch chunks

1 cup green beans, cut into 1-inch lengths

1 cup roasted corn

2 small (underripe) Anjou pears, peeled, cored, and cut into 1-inch chunks

Salt and black pepper to taste

2 tablespoons fresh mint chiffonade

STEPS

- In a small stock pot, cover dried garbanzo beans with water and let soak overnight.
- In a medium-sized sauté pan, heat the olive oil over medium heat. Add the minced garlic and almonds and cook, stirring, for about 2 minutes. Add the onion and cook until soft, about 5 minutes. Add the paprika and tomato paste and stir for a few seconds.
- Add a cup of the stock and bring to a simmer. While you wait for the stock in the sauté pan to simmer, place the garbanzo beans and carrot in a 5-quart pot, add the rest of the stock, and bring to a boil over high heat. Skim any foam off the surface of the stock and discard. Reduce the heat to low.
- Transfer the almond mixture to a food processor and liquefy. Stir this mixture into the soup pot. Add the vinegar and saffron. Cover and cook until the garbanzo beans are soft, about an hour.
- Stir in the pumpkin, green beans, corn and pears, and simmer partially covered for 15 minutes or until pumpkin is soft. Season with salt and pepper.
- Garnish with mint and serve.

Daniel

Some people swear by chicken soup to cure a cold, but in Asturias the favorite home remedy is garlic soup. Garlic soup is thought of as comfort food, a soup to restore health. There's an entire head of garlic in this recipe, but it doesn't really have a "hot" or garlicky flavor. In that way, it is similar to French onion soup, which mellows its sharp-flavored main ingredient with slow caramelization to bring out the sweetest, richest flavors. The garlic taste of this soup is more akin to the savory taste of garlic tucked into a slow-cooking pot roast than the sharp, spicy garlic you would associate with a stir-fry.

Traditionally, this soup might be thickened by adding bread, or enriched by drizzling beaten egg into it as you do with egg drop or Italian wedding soup. But I prefer to assemble these elements together in each bowl as the soup is served: hearty chunks of toasted sourdough on the bottom, topped with an egg poached in the garlic broth, and then the broth ladled gently over all. This preserves the unique textures and flavors of the broth, toast and egg, the better to enjoy them when they are combined with each spoonful.

Garlic Soup

Makes 4–6 servings

INGREDIENTS

10 garlic cloves, peeled and sliced

8 tablespoons olive oil

4–6 slices sourdough bread

4–6 eggs

1 teaspoon pimentón (Spanish smoked paprika)

6 cups chicken stock

2 tablespoons fresh parsley, finely chopped

Salt and pepper to taste

STEPS

- Heat the garlic and oil in a sauté pan slowly over medium-low heat. As it cooks, the garlic will begin to look translucent. When the pieces of garlic turn an opaque white again, you may scoop them out of the oil and set them aside.
- Place the slices of bread in the oil in the bottom of the sauté pan, turning them to toast both sides. Remove and set aside.
- Before returning the garlic to the pan, let the oil cool a bit to avoid the risk of burning the garlic. When the oil is cool enough, add the garlic and the pimentón, stirring them into the oil. Gradually stir in the chicken stock and bring to a simmer. Simmer until the garlic is very soft, 20–30 minutes.
- Use an immersion blender to liquefy the garlic in the stock. Add salt and pepper to taste. Bring back to a simmer.
- While the garlic stock is heating, place a slice of sourdough toast on the bottom of each soup bowl. Poach eggs one at a time in the stock. As each egg is done, remove it from the stock with a skimmer and place it on top of a slice of toast. Pour enough stock into each bowl to cover the toast. Serve topped with chopped parsley.

NOTES

The pimentón in this recipe is Spanish smoked paprika, not just regular Spanish paprika. Pimentón adds a special smoky sweetness.

The most essential instruction for this soup is not to let the garlic get too brown. The garlic is finished cooking when it goes from translucent to opaque white. If it keeps cooking, the garlic may go beyond white to yellowish. This color is fine and the flavor of the garlic will still be good. But if it keeps cooking and has any hint of brown, the garlic is overcooked and will be bitter. In this case, both the garlic and oil will be bitter and should not be used.

Potato Soup

Makes 2–3 servings

INGREDIENTS

2 tablespoons butter

1 large onion, diced

3 pounds russet potatoes, peeled and sliced

Water to cover, 2–3 cups

½ cup whole milk

Salt and pepper to taste

1–2 tablespoons butter

Parsley

STEPS

- Heat the butter in a saucepan. Add the onion and cook until tender. Add the potatoes and cover with water. Bring to a boil and then simmer for about 20 minutes until the potatoes are easily crushed with a fork. Add the milk and continue to simmer for another 10 minutes. Season with salt and pepper.
- Serve with another pat of butter and a little fresh parsley for flavor and eye appeal.

Chris

Just when you think there is nothing in the house to eat, you notice that there are a few potatoes in the bottom of the pantry, and an onion. Combined with a little milk, butter and salt, you have the makings of one of the simplest and most satisfying of dinners. You can scale this recipe up or down depending on the ingredients at hand and the number of servings you'd like. Resist the temptation to blend or whip this soup. That will release the natural starches in the potatoes and result in a pot full of wallpaper paste.

Daniel

Soups have been among my favorite comfort foods since I was little, maybe because they were one of my *abuela's* go-to meals. Sometimes she would add a little sausage to this soup. I have made it with different kinds of beans to see which ones I like best. This is one of those recipes that you will quickly make your own, based on your family's preferences.

Cabbage Soup

Makes 6–8 servings

INGREDIENTS

5 ounces Serrano ham (sliced ¼" thick, if available)

1½ pound beef, top round, uncut

1 onion, diced fine

4 garlic cloves

1 tablespoon olive oil

2 pounds cabbage

2 (15.5-ounce) cans cannellini beans

1 large potato, diced

Salt and pepper to taste

STEPS

- Dice the ham in ¼-inch cubes. Put it in a stock pot together with the whole piece of top round, uncut. Add the onion, garlic cloves, and olive oil and cover with cold water. Bring to a boil and simmer for an hour.
- Remove the beef from the stock pot and set aside. While the beef cools, cut the cabbage in half, remove the core, and chop the cabbage into ¾-inch cubes. Add to the simmering stock. If there is not enough stock to cover the cabbage, add more water. From this point, the soup should probably cook for another 30 minutes, total.
- By now the beef should be a little cooler. Dice the beef into cubes the same size as the ham or perhaps a little larger for variety. Add the beef, beans and diced potato to the simmering stockpot. The soup will be done when the potatoes are soft. Add salt and pepper to taste.

Chris

If you grew up in the 1950s and 1960s you ate a lot of soup from a can. It was inexpensive, easy to prepare, and adaptable to the thousands of recipes that were printed in magazines every week. And to be honest, as I look back on my childhood, tomato soup and a grilled cheese sandwich ranks in the top ten simple pleasures of my memories; even if it was soup from a can. But real tomato soup is within easy reach and it is just as adaptable. The good thing is that you can control the salt and fat content.

Tomato Soup

Makes 2–3 servings

INGREDIENTS

1 (28-ounce) can San Marzano whole peeled Italian tomatoes

1 small onion, diced fine

1 small carrot, diced fine

1 stick celery, diced fine

2 tablespoons olive oil

Salt and pepper to taste

Fresh basil, chopped fine (optional)

STEPS

- Heat the oil in a saucepan and sweat* the vegetables until they are soft and have given up their moisture. The pan will begin to sizzle as they begin to brown.
- Add the entire can of tomatoes with the juice. Bring to a boil and simmer for 20 minutes.
- Use an immersion blender to create a smooth texture. Season with salt and pepper and sprinkle with fresh basil, if using.

* *Sweating is the process of heating and gently stirring diced vegetables in oil or butter to help release the moisture.*

CALL IT MACARONI

Chris – I'm not sure when the American foodies started calling it "pasta," but to us it was all macaroni, from cappellini (angel hair) to pappardelle (broad strips), from tortellini to stuffed shells. And although every macaroni is essentially just a mixture of flour and water or egg, we thought of every variation in size and shape as a separate dish.

Daniel – We didn't eat a lot of pasta growing up, just a couple of specific dishes, but those became some of my favorite comfort foods. Now that I have kids, I have a whole new appreciation for pasta dishes that can not only feed my daughters during (thankfully rare) phases of picky eating, but also satisfy adult palates – becoming our own family favorites.

Chris

In our house, there were some dishes that were made seasonally for Christmas or Lent. Others were based on the availability of ingredients like fresh tomatoes, corn and artichokes, or a windfall of seafood from a fishing excursion. Certain recipes were prepared only once a year on specific dates to honor traditions such as fava beans on December 12 for Santa Lucia and cream puffs on March 19 for San Giuseppe.

But the Sunday Sauce was a tradition that was observed with nearly religious devotion. I can honestly say that over a 30-year period, from my first memories at the table until I was married and making my own sauce, my grandmother never missed a Sunday. That's over 1,500 batches. The aroma of the onions simmering in olive oil followed by the splash of tomatoes being ground into the pan through the foley food mill, and later the intoxicating smell of slightly bitter oregano, the vision of my Gram giving it all a stir with her battered wooden spoon, then tasting to make sure all was right – all these are etched onto my food memory forever.

Sunday Sauce

Makes 2 quarts

INGREDIENTS

3 tablespoons olive oil

1 medium onion, finely diced

2 (28-ounce) cans peeled tomatoes

1 small can tomato paste

1 (28-ounce) can water

4 cloves garlic, peeled

1 tablespoon dried oregano

1 tablespoon dried basil

1 bay leaf

Salt and pepper to taste

STEPS

- In a 4–6 quart sauce pan, heat the oil over medium heat and gently sauté the onions until they are translucent.
- Use a food mill to grind the tomatoes into the pot, leaving the seeds and tough tomato pieces out. This makes for a very smooth and flavorful sauce. Add the tomato paste and one large can of water.
- Crush the garlic cloves slightly under the heel of your hand and add to the sauce along with the oregano, basil and bay leaf. Bring to a boil and lower to a simmer.
- If you're planning to add meat such as meatballs, sausage, or spare ribs cut into pieces, brown the meat and add it to the sauce now. Use a cup or two of sauce to deglaze the browning pan and return the sauce to the pot.
- Continue to simmer for at least 2 hours and as long as four hours. You can partially cover the pot if the sauce is getting too thick.
- It's great with ravioli, spaghetti or any shape of pasta.

Chris

During different stages of my grammar school career at St. Ephrem's in Bay Ridge, Brooklyn, I was in the choir and served as an altar boy. I woke each Sunday morning and headed off with cassock and surplice to sing or serve. When I returned, the Sunday Sauce was about two hours old and the meatballs had been in the sauce for nearly an hour. They were fully cooked and tender but the sauce was still a little thin. Gram would cut open a soft roll and put a meatball on it with a splash of sauce. Then she gently pressed on the meatball to spread it on the roll. That was my Sunday breakfast every week and I can still feel it in my mouth and taste it on my tongue. The longer they cooked in the sauce the more tender they became but the real simple pleasure for me was this pre-dinner treat.

VARIATION

You can put these meatballs on a parchment-paper-lined baking tray and cook at 350°F in the oven for 20 minutes or so, until the internal temperature reaches 160°F.

Meatballs

Makes about 16–20 meatballs

INGREDIENTS

1 egg

½ cup grated Romano cheese

1 cup breadcrumbs

½ cup milk

3 tablespoons minced fresh parsley

1 teaspoon salt

½ teaspoon ground pepper

1 pound lean ground beef

Olive oil for frying

STEPS

- Use a fork to beat the egg and then stir in the cheese, breadcrumbs, milk, parsley and spices. Let the mixture sit for a few minutes so the bread crumbs will absorb the liquid.
- Crumble the meat into the bowl and gently stir with a fork until the mixture is uniform.
- Wet your hands and grab about 2 tablespoons of meat. (Less or more depending on your preference). Press the meat into a ball and gently roll between your palms into a uniform ball.
- Heat ¼-inch olive oil in a frying pan and add the meatballs. Keep turning until brown on all sides and then add to the sauce.

At some point, Gram decided that I was old enough to be given the task of shaping the meatballs before they were fried and put in the sauce. Of course, she still mixed the egg, milk, cheese and breadcrumbs with the meat and parsley, but my job was to scoop up a small amount in my hands and roll it into a perfectly round, smooth ball. I was so proud of my handiwork as I surveyed the tray of meatballs, until Gram came over and pointed at one of the smaller balls. "Who's going to get this one?" When I shrugged, she said, "What if one of our guests gets it and sees that everyone else has a bigger meatball?" Once more I shrugged and she scooped up all the meatballs, put the mixture back in the bowl and said, "Try again!" Lesson learned.

Pesto

Makes 1½ cups

INGREDIENTS

2 cups fresh basil packed into the cups (or 4 cubes frozen)

1–2 cloves garlic

¾ cup grated Romano cheese

¼ cup toasted pignolia nuts (or toasted walnut pieces)

½ – ¾ cup olive oil

STEPS

- Place the basil, garlic, cheese and nuts in the bowl of a food processor. Add ½ cup of the olive oil and process until smooth.
- Add enough additional oil to create a cream-like consistency. Avoid running the machine for a long time to prevent a heat build-up that could affect the basil.

Chris

There were just two herbs in my childhood cooking experience: dried oregano and fresh basil. The oregano went into all kinds of sauces and the basil was omnipresent with tomatoes and mozzarella. But because my family's food tradition was from Sicily, we never had pesto. Now it is a staple in our house for a quick pasta dish (especially hearty homemade cuts like gnocchi and cavatelli), and as a seasoning for chicken, fish and even lamb.

TIP

Each summer I harvest the basil from the plants in our yard and put it in the food processor with a little olive oil. Once it is smooth I pour the mixture into ice cube trays and freeze them for a few hours. Then I pop out the cubes to store in a freezer bag. All winter I have access to "fresh" basil for pesto.

Chris

I just love the name of this simple pasta dish that is enjoyed in every restaurant in Rome. It sounds like the name of an Italian comedy duo (think Martin and Lewis or Abbott and Costello from days gone by). But in reality it is a recipe that brings out the flavors and textures of the cheese and pasta. I like to serve this with a type of macaroni called bucatini, or perciatelli. They are both hearty pastas that stand up to the bold flavors of the cheese and pepper.

Cacio e Pepe (Cheese and Pepper)

Makes 4–6 servings

INGREDIENTS

1 pound bucatini or perciatelli pasta

4 tablespoons butter

1 cup grated Parmigiano Reggiano cheese

½ cup grated Romano cheese

2 teaspoons freshly cracked pepper

STEPS

- Cook the pasta in 6 quarts of boiling, salted water until just one minute before al dente. (The pasta will finish cooking in the sauce.) Drain the pasta and reserve about 2 cups of the cooking water.
- Melt the butter in a large skillet. Then turn off the heat and add the drained pasta, cheese, pepper and the cooking water. Stir briskly until a cheesy sauce coats the pasta.
- Serve immediately with more grated cheese and fresh black pepper.

Chris

Many of my favorite recipes from childhood were actually dishes of necessity. In the South they might be referred to as "soul food," and we have the same loyalty to these dishes. Mom was always trying to figure out how to stretch her meagre food allowance to provide three meals a day to our family of six. Capellini (angel hair) is the finest of the spaghetti strands and it cooks up in just 2 or 3 minutes. If you leave out the zucchini, this garlic infused olive oil dressing is called aglio e olio – garlic and oil.

LEFTOVERS TIP

If there should ever be any of this pasta left over the next day (which will be rare), you can beat an egg or two with some grated cheese, stir in the leftover pasta and then fry in a nonstick skillet until brown and crisp on both sides.

Pasta Cucuzza

Makes 4–6 servings

INGREDIENTS

¼ cup olive oil

4 cloves garlic, peeled

4 small zucchini

1 pound angel hair pasta

Grated Romano cheese

STEPS

- Heat the oil in a large, high-sided skillet. Add the garlic cloves.
- Slice the zucchini in ¼-inch rounds and fry in single-layer batches until well browned on both sides. Then put them in the large bowl you will be using for the finished pasta.
- Cook the pasta in boiling salted water until just before al dente. This pasta only takes a minute or two after the water returns to a boil. Use tongs to transfer the pasta to the skillet and toss the pasta with the remaining oil in the pan.
- Pour the pasta into the large bowl with the zucchini slices and serve with mountains of freshly grated Romano cheese.

Fresh Pasta

Makes 1 pound or 4 servings

INGREDIENTS

2 cups flour/durum/ semolina (or a mixture)

1 teaspoon salt

2 eggs

1 teaspoon olive oil

¼ cup water

STEPS

- Put the flour(s), salt, eggs and oil into the bowl of the processor. Pulse the machine until the mixture forms a ball. If it is too dry, sprinkle in some water, a teaspoon at a time, until it forms a smooth dough that cleans the side of the bowl.
- Remove the dough and knead it a few times to create a smooth ball. Wrap in plastic and let rest for an hour or so, then roll out into the shapes you want. An easy way to do this is to cut the dough into four pieces and roll each out on a floured board until it is as flat as you can get it.
- For linguini and other similar shapes, sprinkle some flour on the top and roll up into a tight cylinder. Slice the cylinder into rounds and then unfurl the linguini.
- Boil the pasta gently in simmering water for just a few minutes. Fresh pasta does not have to cook nearly as long as dried pasta.
- Enjoy with your favorite sauce or just some butter and grated Romano cheese.

Chris

Homemade pasta is one of those revelations in the kitchen, as in, "You mean that's all there is to making your own pasta?" This dough is very versatile. You can use it for a variety of shapes – like linguini (thin strips), pappardelle (wide strips), or farfalle (bow ties), as well as for stuffed pasta like tortellini, ravioli and cannelloni. I especially like to use fresh pasta to assemble lasagna since there is no need to boil the pasta beforehand.

ABOUT FLOUR

The texture of the pasta is improved by the use of either durum wheat or semolina as part or all of the mixture. For regular pasta I favor all semolina. For filled pasta, a mixture of half and half gives a softer texture that is easier to manipulate. Traditional pasta is made by cracking eggs into a well of flour and then mixing it together until the dough forms. This is one recipe where a food processor makes quick work of the job and provides a smooth, even dough. Use the dough blade if you have one.

Chris

Most of my family food memories come from my mother's side of the family. We grew up in my grandmother's house and she was the chef-in-charge. But this handmade pasta is from my father's side of the family. Aunt Mary and Aunt Mamie were the two oldest sisters in a family of eight kids, so they were accustomed to recipes that could feed a small horde of hungry men. I remember them rolling the little pellets on the inside of a cheese grater to create the bumpy texture and then laying them out on a clean sheet to dry. I never had a chance to ask them for a recipe for the dough, but this is simply a variation on the standard fresh pasta mixture. The difference comes from the addition of ricotta cheese, which makes it more supple and rich.

FOR AUTHENTIC CAVATELLI

The true cavatelli shape requires rolling each little cooked "pellet" on the back of a cheese grater or cavatelli board to create the traditional ridged curl. And then spreading them out to dry – the way my dear aunts did.

Cavatelli

Makes 1 pound or 4 servings

INGREDIENTS

2 cups semolina

1 egg

1 cup ricotta

½ teaspoon salt

¼ cup of water

STEPS

- Add the all the ingredients except the water into the bowl of a food processor fitted with the dough blade. Pulse until a smooth dough forms and cleans the side of the bowl. If the mixture seems too dry, sprinkle water a teaspoon at a time.
- Take the dough out and knead it a few times to form a smooth ball. Wrap in plastic and let rest for an hour or so.
- Divide the dough into 8 pieces. Roll each piece on a floured board until it is a long, pencil-thick cylinder. Cut the cylinders into ½-inch pieces.
- At this point you can just throw these into some simmering water and cook them until they float to the surface of the pot.

Chris

This is another fresh pasta that was not a part of my family tradition. I first experienced it during a summer job as a waiter at an Italian resort in the Catskills called the Villa Vosilla. The chef was a giant of a man who had cooked for both the Italian and American armies. He was the first professional cook I had ever observed and he was amazing in his breadth of knowledge and incredible technique. I remember that for one dish he had to completely debone a chicken, a task he could perform in less than one minute! He made the gnocchi directly on the marble work top using his enormous chef's knife to mince, mash and blend all the ingredients into the proper texture. This recipe takes advantage of the food processor to achieve the fluffy pasta pillows.

Gnocchi

Makes 4 servings

INGREDIENTS

2 cups potatoes, cooked, peeled and riced (or mashed)

2 eggs, beaten

1 clove garlic, minced

½ teaspoon salt

¼ teaspoon black pepper

1 cup semolina (plus more for dusting)

STEPS

- Put all the ingredients into the food processor and pulse to mix. If the dough seems too dry you can drizzle in a teaspoon of water at a time until the dough just comes together. Pulse a few more times and empty the dough onto a flour-dusted work surface.
- Gently fold the dough until it is light and smooth. Don't overwork the dough.
- Cut the dough into 8 pieces and roll each piece into a rope about ½-inch thick. Cut each rope into ¾-inch pieces and transfer to a flour-dusted baking sheet until all the pieces are formed.
- Drop the gnocchi into boiling salted water and stir very gently. Once the gnocchi have floated to the top, cook them another minute and then drain.
- Serve with the sauce of your choice or just a little butter and grated cheese.

ABOUT GRATED CHEESE

There are basically two types of hard Italian cheeses that are used for grating. The first group is made from cow's milk. These include the more generic Parmesan, named after the region around the city of Parma where the cheese originated. Then there is Parmigiano Reggiano, which is an appellation that is strictly controlled and applied only to cheeses made in that specific region. These cheeses have a nutty taste and superior melting qualities.

The other cheese is Pecorino, so named because they are made from sheep's milk and the Italian word for sheep is "pecora." The most famous of these cheeses is Pecorino Romano, named because of its popularity in that region. The cheese is usually very sharp and noticeably saltier than the cow's milk counterpart. Very often the cheese is simply referred to as Romano cheese, but there are as many pecorino cheeses as there are regions in Italy: Pecorino Toscano, Pecorino Siciliano, etc.

SPOILER ALERT

American-made cheeses called Romano are made with cow's milk.

Macarrones con Chorizo (Penne Pasta with Chorizo Sausage)

Makes 6 servings

INGREDIENTS

1 tablespoon olive oil

1 medium-size yellow onion, finely diced

5 chorizo sausages sliced into ¼-inch rounds

1¼-inch-thick slice Serrano ham (or prosciutto) diced, about 5 ounces

1 (26- to 29-ounce) can tomato sauce

Salt to taste

1 pound penne pasta or mostaccioli pasta

Parmigiano Reggiano cheese, grated, for garnish

STEPS

- Start heating water for the pasta. Set a 6-quart saucepan of water on high heat and add a large pinch of salt. Cover the saucepan and begin making the sauce.
- Heat olive oil on medium heat in a large pan. (To complete this recipe you will stir the cooked penne into the sauce, so choose a pan that gives you enough room to combine the pasta and sauce together.) Add the diced onion and sauté until translucent. Add chorizo sausage rounds and cook for 2 more minutes. Mix in the Serrano ham and sauté for one more minute.
- Pour in the tomato sauce and heat it to a simmer. Chorizo and ham can be quite salty, so be sure to taste before adding any salt. Let the sauce simmer until the pasta is done, about 10 minutes.
- The pasta water should be boiling by now. Cook the penne as the packaging recommends for al dente pasta (still firm). Drain the pasta and combine it with the sauce in the large pan.
- Remove from heat and serve with grated Parmigiano cheese.

Daniel

As a child, I spent hours watching my grandmother cook. Sitting at the kitchen table with my sketchpad, I would watch her everyday movement through the kitchen as if it were the most marvelous of shows. Washing, prepping and chopping of ingredients seemed to happen all at once, all in silence. We didn't need to talk. Sometimes, when she was in the middle of a familiar routine, I would take my eyes away from her hands, but only to draw a picture of her cooking.

One day – I don't remember how old I was, maybe 10 or 12 – my grandmother let me make this dish. Life was forever changed. Everything before that moment became "before I could cook."

The dish was Macarrones con Chorizo, a simple kids' meal that I still enjoy to this day.

Chris

When I think of baked macaroni and cheese it has nothing to do with elbow noodles and chunks of Velveeta. It's all about the bubbly, delicious resurrection of Sunday's pasta in a deep dish casserole – a kind of free-form lasagna with the ziti or rigatoni filling in for the pasta layers. If you are making this from scratch, you can cook the noodles a little less than al dente so that they can finish during the baking process. But if you are using leftover pasta, don't worry, it will be delicious.

Maccheroni al Forno (Baked Macaroni)

Makes 6–8 servings

INGREDIENTS

1 pound macaroni (penne, rigatoni, fusilli, etc.)

3 pounds ricotta

½ cup grated Romano cheese, divided

1 tablespoon fresh parsley, chopped

Salt and pepper to taste

1 pound fresh mozzarella

1 quart tomato sauce (see Sunday Sauce, page 64)

STEPS

- Preheat the oven to 350°F.
- Cook the pasta in 6 quarts of salted water until just a minute before it is al dente (firm). Drain.
- Mix the ricotta with ¼ cup of the grated cheese and the freshly chopped parsley, and salt and pepper to taste.
- Chop the mozzarella into small chunks.
- Spread 1½ cups of the tomato sauce in the bottom of a deep casserole dish. Add a layer of pasta followed by a layer of ½ of the ricotta mixture and ⅓ of the mozzarella. Add another layer of pasta followed by 1 cup of the sauce, the rest of the ricotta mixture and another ⅓ of the mozzarella.
- Add the final layer of pasta and then sauce, and sprinkle the remaining mozzarella on top followed by the remaining Romano cheese.
- Bake for 30 minutes until bubbly and the cheese top has begun to brown. Let it sit for 10 minutes until it has a chance to settle.

Chris

It's not uncommon for Southern Italians to refer to Northern Italians as "polenta eaters." This cornmeal mush was the staple of the northern diet the way pasta was in the south. Although it was not part of our table when I was growing up, I have come to enjoy the deep comfort from its creamy texture and its ability to highlight the flavors of even the most humble toppings.

Polenta

Makes 4 servings

INGREDIENTS

2 cups milk

2 cups water

1 teaspoon salt

1 cup cornmeal or polenta (not the quick cook variety)

2 tablespoons butter

½ cup grated Romano cheese

STEPS

- Heat the milk, water and salt in a large saucepan. Just before the mixture comes to a boil, sprinkle in the cornmeal while whisking vigorously. This is the hardest part of the whole recipe.
- Once the cornmeal has all been added, lower the temp to a simmer and switch to a wooden spoon. Stir gently, making sure to get into the corners of the pan so the bottom doesn't burn.
- Cook for 15–20 minutes until the mixture thickens and starts to leave the side of the pan when you stir.
- Add the butter and cheese and serve immediately.
- You can also pour the polenta into a buttered loaf pan and let it cool. Turn the loaf out on a cutting board and cut into 1-inch slices, then fry the slices in a little butter or olive oil until they are browned on both sides.

Fideuà

Makes 8 servings

INGREDIENTS

4 cups chicken stock

¼ teaspoon saffron

2 tablespoon olive oil

1 small onion, finely diced

1 green pepper, finely diced

1 red pepper, finely diced

3 garlic cloves, minced

1 carrot, diced

1 tablespoon tomato paste

1 fryer chicken, cut up into 8 pieces

1 pound fideo pasta

1 cup green peas

8–10 prawns (optional)

Salt and pepper to taste

STEPS

- Bring chicken stock to a simmer in a saucepan. Add saffron. Cover and remove from heat.
- Heat the olive oil in a paella pan or cast iron frying pan and sauté the onion, peppers, garlic and carrot for about 6 minutes until softened, stirring often. Mix in the tomato paste and chicken pieces. Cook the chicken for 6–8 minutes on each side, stirring constantly to prevent the vegetables from burning.
- Add the pasta and stir into the chicken and vegetables. Cook for 1 minute. Pour in the hot chicken stock and stir, making sure all the pasta is mostly covered. Cook uncovered according to the pasta instructions, usually 6–8 minutes, during which time the liquid should mostly disappear.
- *(Optional)* Add prawns at this point if you are using them.
- Remove the pan from the heat and let the fideuá rest for 5 minutes before serving.

Daniel

Fideuà is one of the few traditional pasta dishes of Spain. It's similar to paella, but made with pasta instead of rice. Even though everybody knows paella as the most Spanish of dishes, fideuà has a healthy following of its own in the Valencia and Barcelona regions of Spain. Fideuà can be thrown together and cooked much faster than paella, making it a traditional Spanish "fast food" that's a good choice for busy families.

This dish gets its name from fideo pasta. It's like spaghetti, but short – less than an inch long. If you can't find any at your store, break up spaghetti into pieces 1–1½ inches long. Fideuà is traditionally made with seafood. I make this all-chicken version with my kids in mind, but from time to time I will add some seafood for the grownups, as you can see in the photo.

If you don't have a paella pan, a large cast iron frying pan will work just fine.

THE EGG AND US

Chris – When I was young we ate eggs all the time. We even had an eggman (Roy) who delivered eggs just like the milkman. Every pantry was stocked with egg cups that held one soft boiled egg on top and one kept warm below. We dipped our toast in the runny yolks and enjoyed every delicious bite of that simple pleasure. Then came the cholesterol scare and eggs became a rare treat. Now that the cholesterol facts have been straightened out and we learn that eggs are an economical and healthy source of protein, it seems we are free to enjoy this simple pleasure again for breakfast, lunch or dinner.

Daniel – Have you ever heard somebody who lacks confidence or experience in the kitchen say they "can't even boil water?" The Spanish version of that expression is "can't even fry an egg!" Eggs are very special to us kitchen folk: a humble ingredient, typically one of the first things you learn to cook yourself at home, and one that remains a staple ingredient in even the fanciest preparations throughout your kitchen career. Some will tell you that the number of pleats in a chef's toque shows how many ways the chef can prepare an egg, but that's nonsense – no hat could hold that many pleats.

Chris

The greatest deterrent to people trying recipes that include hard boiled eggs is the fact that no one seems to have solved the mystery of how to boil an egg so that the yolk is bright and yellow with no surrounding grey area, the whites are firm but not rubbery, and, most important, the eggs release from their shells without a lot of swearing and hair-pulling. Weep no more. This method is simple and effective.

The first thing to know is that older eggs peel better. It has to do with the egg/air relationship inside the shell. So, buy the eggs a week before you want to boil them.

Hard Boiled Eggs

INGREDIENTS

Desired number of eggs

STEPS

- Place the desired number of eggs into a saucepan and cover them with at least 2 inches of cold water. Place the pan over medium-high heat and bring to a boil. As soon as the water has come to a full boil, take the pan off the heat and cover.
- Set the timer for 12 minutes.
- Then pour out the hot water and give the eggs a vigorous shake to crack the shells. Fill the pan with cold water, drain and fill with more cold water. Now the eggs should be cool enough to handle.
- Peel them under cold running water. The shells should come off easily.
- You can store the peeled eggs for several days in the refrigerator.

Egg Salad

Makes 2 cups

INGREDIENTS

6 hard boiled eggs, peeled and chopped

6 tablespoons mayonnaise

1 teaspoon mustard

1 green onion, finely chopped

Salt and pepper to taste

STEPS

- Chop the eggs as finely or coarsely as you like.
- Mix with the mayonnaise, mustard and green onion, and season with salt and pepper.

Chris

The prime season for egg salad is probably the week or two after Easter as we all try to think of ways to use the dozens of colored eggs from our children's baskets. But this creamy salad is a welcome find in sandwiches and on crackers at any time of year.

When there were such things as luncheonettes, I used to enjoy the salad platter that included a scoop each of egg, tuna and potato salad on a bed of iceberg lettuce served with melba toast crackers. At the time I probably ordered it because it was the least expensive option on the menu, but now it is a special treat.

Chris

Although deviled eggs were staples of American entertaining in the 1950s, their origins go back as far as ancient Rome. The actual term starts to appear in the 18th century and we've enjoyed these spicy eggs ever since. And what's not to like? You can whip up a batch of these delectable bites to bring to a party for less than the price of a bag of chips!

Deviled Eggs

Makes 24 deviled egg halves

INGREDIENTS

12 hard boiled eggs, cut in half lengthwise

¼ cup mayonnaise

¼ cup ketchup

1 teaspoon Dijon mustard

¼ teaspoon cayenne pepper

½ teaspoon salt

Paprika for sprinkling

STEPS

- Remove the egg yolks to a mixing bowl and put the white halves on a tray, cut side up.
- Mix the mayonnaise, ketchup and mustard into the yolks with a whisk until the mixture is smooth.
- Season with salt and cayenne, then spoon into the egg white halves. Sprinkle the tops with paprika.

Eggs Poached in Peas

Makes 6 servings

INGREDIENTS

2 tablespoons olive oil

1 onion, finely diced

1 quart chicken broth

1 pound frozen peas

6 eggs

Salt and freshly cracked pepper to taste

Grated Romano cheese

STEPS

- For this dish you need a large covered sauté pan. Heat the oil over medium heat and sauté the onion until it is soft but not browned. Add the chicken broth and bring to a boil. Add the peas and wait for the broth to come back to a boil.
- Use the back of a large spoon or ladle to make six indentations in the peas. Gently crack an egg into each of the indentations.
- Lower the heat to a simmer and cover tightly. Cook for 8 minutes or until the eggs are firm.
- Serve with salt and pepper to taste and a healthy grating of Romano cheese.

Chris

Now that you have that chicken stock in the freezer there is a whole world of simple pleasures that will be made delicious by the incorporation of that liquid gold (recipe on page 38).

Growing up, we observed meatless meals on Fridays and many nights of the Lenten season. My mom got very creative with egg and vegetable combinations. For us, it was not a deprivation but a chance to experience some of our favorite foods, dishes I think about all year long.

Daniel

The formal name for this quick meal is arroz a la Cubana (Cuban-style rice), but most people just call it arroz con huevos (rice and eggs). In Spain, it is often made for dinner, which is typically smaller and simpler than lunch, but you can serve this for lunch or even a hearty breakfast. There are many variations of this dish. This recipe is for the basic version that we ate most often.

The recipe calls for 2 cups of tomato sauce to be made ahead of time. Tomate frito is a perfect fit, but any of the homemade sauces will work well. If you haven't had time to make your own sauce, don't worry. Canned sauce will do. Look for crushed tomatoes prepared without any seasonings like oregano, garlic, and so forth. Plain crushed tomatoes are a good staple to have on hand. You can season them to suit whatever meal you are making.

If you have mastered the basics, this dish will be magic, with each flavor and texture distinct but complementing the others. With each mouthful, you will savor the yolk tempering the tomato sauce, blending together in a creamy counterpoint to the garlicky grains of rice. Each forkful will be a struggle to assemble the perfect ratio of components until the very final bite.

Arroz con Huevos (Rice with Fried Eggs)

Makes 4 servings

INGREDIENTS

2 tablespoons olive oil (approx.), plus more for frying the eggs

2 garlic cloves

2 cups jasmine rice

4 cups water

1 teaspoon salt (optional)

2 cups tomato sauce (recommended: plain homemade marinara sauce)

4 eggs

Salt and pepper to taste

STEPS

- Heat about 2 tablespoons of oil in a saucepan over medium heat. Cut both garlic cloves in half and sauté them lightly in the oil for 1–2 minutes, until you really notice the delicious garlic aroma rising from the pan.
- Add the rice to the saucepan, stirring and cooking for a couple of minutes. Add the water and a teaspoon of salt (optional). Reduce heat to low and simmer for 15 minutes.
- While the rice is simmering, heat the tomato sauce.
- When the rice is done, the sauce should be hot and it's time to start frying the eggs.

  Note: You will plate and serve each egg as soon as it is done. The eggs may be "sunny-side up" or "over easy," but be careful not to cook them too much – a runny yolk is an important feature of this dish.
- Fry the eggs one at a time in olive oil over medium-low heat. Just when the egg is a moment or two from being done, fluff the rice in the pot and place a big scoop on one plate. Quickly spoon tomato sauce over the rice.
- Slide the perfectly fried egg on top of the rice and serve to the hungriest person. No one wants to hear cranky whining when they are standing over a hot stove! Start frying another egg immediately while everything is nice and hot.
- Get another plate: rice, sauce, egg. Do this twice more and the chef can sit down to eat.

Daniel

The tortilla de patata, or Spanish potato omelet, has to be the most traditional Spanish dish. If you travel throughout Spain, you'll find many different regional recipes for tortilla de patata, but any Spaniard will tell you that the best version is the one they make at home.

The basic version is a very simple recipe, calling for just potatoes, onion, eggs, and a little salt. Plus the olive oil that you cook it in. That's it. So why are there so many different versions? Because everyone wants to put their stamp on it and make it their own.

For example, everybody who makes a tortilla de patata has their own preference for how the potatoes should be cut: thick slices, thin slices, cubes, and so on. Some people use only the essential ingredients, while others might like to add a little garlic, chorizo, aromatic herbs, or any imaginable delicious combination. Any customization you can think of for a frittata would be good for a tortilla de patata, too.

In the recipe I explain how to make the most basic tortilla de patata. I leave it up to your taste and imagination to change it as you go. Making it this way at first will allow you later on to decide what else you would do or add to it.

Tortilla de Patata (Potato Omelet)

Makes 6 servings

INGREDIENTS

1½ cups olive oil

1 large onion

2 large potatoes

Salt to taste

2 garlic cloves

7 eggs

Nonstick cooking spray (optional)

STEPS

- Begin heating olive oil in a nonstick 10-inch sauté pan over medium heat. Peel and dice the onion and add it to the oil. While the oil keeps heating, peel, dice, and salt the potatoes. When oil comes up to a medium-high heat, reduce heat, stir to prevent onions from sticking to the bottom of the pan, and add the potatoes. Chop garlic coarsely and add it to the pan. Stir from time to time to make sure nothing sticks to the pan.
- Break the eggs into a medium-sized bowl, season with salt and whisk lightly.
- Keep testing the potatoes. The moment they begin to turn soft, turn off the heat and use a skimmer to transfer them to the egg mixture, draining away as much oil as you can.
- Pour oil out of the sauté pan until only about ½ tablespoon of oil remains. Tilt the pan from side to side and all around until the cooking surface is coated with oil. If you are using cooking spray, spray the pan. Spoon the potato-and-egg mixture evenly into the pan. Let it cook slowly at medium-low heat. You will see the edges of the tortilla finish cooking first. The tortilla should be ready to flip in 15 minutes.

- Put a 10-inch plate face down on top of the pan. With one hand grasping the handle of the sauté pan and the other pressing the plate firmly against the pan, flip the pan and plate over together so that the tortilla falls out onto the plate. Quickly slide the tortilla from the plate back into the sauté pan. If you flipped the tortilla successfully, you will be filled with euphoria. Remain focused. Press the edges of the tortilla down with a fork so that they make full contact with the pan.
- Continue cooking over low heat for another 10–15 minutes, just enough time to take photos and start bragging about your accomplishment on social media. When a cake tester or toothpick comes out clean, the tortilla is done! Put a clean plate face down on the pan and repeat the tortilla flipping maneuver.
- Serve warm or at room temperature.

TIP

Flipping the tortilla de patata requires some practice. Your first attempt may be a little messy, even if you have a really great nonstick pan. Cooking spray can provide a little extra help. If you lose some of the tortilla, don't feel bad. It has happened to me before, and I'm sure it will happen again. Have fun and *buen provecho!*

Béchamel Omelets

Makes 8-10 servings

SAUCE

INGREDIENTS

1 stick butter, or 8 tablespoons

1 small onion, finely diced

1 garlic clove, minced

10 tablespoons flour

8 ounces Serrano ham, diced (optional)

8 ounces cauliflower, blanched, drained and cut into small pieces

4 cups milk at room temperature

Parsley

Salt to taste

STEPS

- Melt the butter in a large sauté pan. Add the onion and garlic, and "sweat" them for a couple of minutes (gently cooking to let them release their liquids). Stir in the flour and cook for another 2–3 minutes. Add the ham and/or cauliflower to the pan.
- Now it's time for the milk. If you dump it all in at once, you'll have nothing but lumps. Instead, slowly pour in a little stream of milk, stirring continually. Pause the stream of milk to let the mixture heat up, but keep stirring. When the mixture seems to be getting hot, maybe showing a few bubbles at the edges, add just a little more milk and keep stirring.
- Cook the béchamel for approximately 20 minutes altogether, stirring all the while. You should now have a creamy sauce.
- Sprinkle in the parsley and season with salt.
- At this point, you may choose to spoon some of the béchamel over buttered toast points for a little snack. Professionals call this "quality control."

(continued)

Daniel

Béchamel croquettes (croquetas in Spanish) are one of my favorite comfort foods. Crispy on the outside and creamy on the inside, they are a wonderful savory treat. Even less known than croquettes are béchamel omelets, which have all the "comfort" value of a croquette, folded inside beaten eggs to make a quick and nourishing meal. My grandmother used to make these omelets for us using a béchamel with cauliflower or sometimes ham or chicken. We loved them! This may be a way to get your kids to eat cauliflower, too.

The béchamel filling requires some practice and planning. It is always better to make it the day before. And always err on the side of cooking it more rather than less to obtain a thicker filling. Thick béchamel is easier to work with in croquettes or omelets. Just be careful not to burn it – the smell of burned milk is the worst!

Refrigerate sauce overnight and use in croquettes or omelets.

SAUCE STEPS (continued)

- Pour the sauce from the pan into a container where it can spread to no more than 1 inch thick.
- Cover with plastic wrap, smoothing the wrap right onto the surface of the sauce so that it doesn't form a skin. Refrigerate overnight.
- When the béchamel is cold, you can cut and shape it into croquettes or use it in slices to fill an omelet.

OMELET

INGREDIENTS

2 eggs per omelet

Salt and pepper to taste

Olive oil

STEPS

- Crack eggs into a bowl. Add a pinch of salt and pepper before whisking with a fork or a whisk until the white and the yolk are fully blended.
- Bring your pan to a high heat and add oil so that the mixture doesn't stick (using a nonstick pan is great for these, too). Pour in your mixture and cook on a high heat for 2 minutes, making sure the mixture is spread out evenly.
- As the egg begins to set, use a spatula to push the set egg towards the center of the omelet.
- Add about a half cup of bechamel down the center of the omelet. Cook the omelet for another minute, then loosen the edges with a spatula and fold the omelet in half.
- Tilt the pan and slide the omelet onto a plate. Serve immediately.

Rocky Mountain Toast

Makes 1 serving

INGREDIENTS

1 tablespoon butter, divided

1 slice thick bread

1 egg

Salt and pepper to taste

STEPS

- Melt half the butter in a skillet over medium heat.
- Use a biscuit cutter (or drinking glass) to remove a 2-inch circle from the center of the bread.
- Place the bread into the pan and crack the egg directly into the hole. Cook until the egg has started to get firm and the bread is browned on the bottom. Lift the bread and egg out of the pan with a spatula and place the remaining butter in the pan.
- Turn the bread over to cook the second side. When the egg is as firm as you like, remove to a plate and season with salt and pepper.

Chris

You won't find the this recipe in any cookbook or encyclopedia. That's because the name was invented by my daughter Sharon. I think she had some version of the dish at camp and wanted me to duplicate it at home. I love making this dish with and for kids and I make it for myself to stimulate memories of that little girl who used to live in my house and now is a mother herself.

Chris

This was a favorite lunch of mine in my early school days. Mom would fry the peppers with some leftover boiled potatoes and then bring it all together with the addition of the eggs. Great just the way it is and phenomenal in a sandwich. This recipe is best (and easiest) when it is made from leftovers, but you can make it from scratch.

Peppers, Potatoes and Eggs

Makes 1–2 servings

INGREDIENTS

3–4 sweet Italian peppers

Olive oil

1 large Idaho potato

2 eggs, beaten

Salt and pepper to taste

STEPS

- Remove the stems and seeds from the peppers and cut into long strips about 1 inch wide. Put a little olive oil in a frying pan and sauté the peppers until they are tender and lightly browned.
- Peel the potato and cut into 1-inch cubes. Boil them in water until they are tender (about 10 minutes). Drain.
- Add the cooked potatoes to the peppers and sauté for a few minutes, until the potatoes start to brown around the edges.
- Pour the eggs into the pan and stir with a wooden spoon or silicone spatula until the eggs are cooked to your liking. Season with salt and pepper and serve.

Revuelto

Makes 1 serving

INGREDIENTS

1 tablespoon green onions, sliced

1 tablespoon olive oil

6–8 salad shrimp

1 egg

Salt and pepper to taste

Pimentón (smoked paprika) to taste

STEPS

- Clean and slice the green onions on a bias into ¼-inch pieces. Pour olive oil into a nonstick sauté pan over medium heat. Add the green onions and sauté for about a minute.
- Add shrimp and cook for 2 minutes.
- Crack the egg directly into the sauté pan. (If you are concerned that you may get eggshells into the pan, crack the egg into a small bowl first and then pour into the pan.)
- Gently stir the egg with a wooden spoon or silicone spatula just until the egg begins to set – a minute or less. Season to taste with salt, pepper,and a dash of pimentón.

Daniel

Scrambled eggs are a tasty option all on their own. And as we see in Chris' recipe Peppers, Potatoes and Eggs (page 106), they unite a few simple ingredients into a great "comfort food" dish.

Revueltos are a version of this comfort food that I grew up with. They embody this approach of taking a few ingredients that are already on hand, scrambling them with an egg and making it a meal. For example, if you have a few of Chris' Mushrooms Marsala (page 140) left over, they would make a great mushroom revuelto.

Revuelto simply means "scrambled." This shrimp revuelto (revuelto de gambas) is very typical, something you might be served in a restaurant in Spain, as well as at a kitchen table – and it's great for a breakfast or snack.

Chris

Can we talk about the pantry? It's the most important aspect of your kitchen. More important than gadgets and appliances. And all it takes is a little planning to make sure that you always have the ingredients on hand to turn out simple and delicious meals. Even in an era when freezer compartments were so small they could barely hold a few ice trays, my mother always kept a box or two of frozen spinach. In the fridge there were eggs, cream cheese, butter and Romano cheese. I now realize that Mom made spinach pie on nights when the day had been too hectic for more extensive shopping and preparation. At the time I thought she only made it because we all loved it so much.

Spinach Pie

Makes 4 servings

INGREDIENTS

3–4 eggs

4 ounces cream cheese

4 tablespoons grated Romano cheese

1 package frozen spinach, thawed and drained

1 tablespoon butter

¼ cup breadcrumbs

STEPS

- Preheat the oven to 350°F.
- Beat the eggs, cream cheese and Romano together until smooth. Add the spinach and mix well.
- Grease a 6-inch pie plate or small casserole dish with the butter and sprinkle with breadcrumbs to coat the bottom and sides. Pour in spinach mixture and bake for approximately 30 minutes.
- We often include one or more additional cheeses to make the dish more of a quiche. You can try mozzarella, feta or cheddar. Sliced black olives give it a Mediterranean flair.

FAMILY FAVORITES

We have gone into our family memory banks to pull out a few of our personal favorites. You should make a list of your own Family Favorites, write them down on index cards and stick them in this section of the book. This way you will not only make the recipes your own but the book as well.

There are many times when favorite family recipes are anything but simple. They may bring back great memories of favorite meals and favorite people, but they include hours or even days of preparation. And there are many times when family traditions, however warm a memory they conjure, fall outside the boundaries of what can be commonly considered as tasty – like putting mayonnaise on popcorn for example. It may be a fondly remembered family pleasure but not one to be shared.

Daniel

In Asturias, the province of Spain where I was born and raised, cider is close to a religion.

When you walk by any outdoor celebration in Asturias – or even if you're just walking by a cider pub on an ordinary day – the fruity, smoky aroma of chorizo being cooked in cider permeates the air. Just thinking about it gives me cravings. And I think about it often! When I get these cravings, I cook up some chorizo in apple cider.

This makes a great appetizer, hearty and savory, with a tangy sauce for dipping bread. The chorizo sausage doesn't have to be made in Spain nor the cider in Asturias – the results will still be good. You could even use non-alcoholic cider. When most of the cider has been cooked off, I sometimes add a few slices of a Granny Smith apple. While you and your guests are trying to decide whether you prefer the chorizo slices or the apple slices, you will polish off the whole dish.

It pairs well with cider, of course.

Chorizo a la Sidra (Sausage in Cider)

Makes 6–8 servings

INGREDIENTS

6-8 chorizo sausages

3 cups apple cider, alcoholic (hard) or non-alcoholic

1 Granny Smith apple, cored, peeled and sliced in wedges (optional)

STEPS

- Put the chorizo sausages in a sauté pan and cover with the apple cider. Cook uncovered on low heat until most of the cider evaporates, about an hour. Shake the pan from time to time, especially as the cider becomes thicker and caramelizes.
- When most of the cider has evaporated, add slices of apple if desired and cook for the final 5 minutes.
- To serve, spoon sausage over slices of fresh, crusty bread.

Arroz con Salchichas (Rice with Sausage and Ribs)

Makes 6 servings

INGREDIENTS

1 pound sausage (Spanish style salchichas frescas or sweet Italian sausage)

1 large onion, diced

1 large red bell pepper, diced

2 tablespoons olive oil

Salt for seasoning the ribs

1 rack pork ribs, cut in half and separated

3 cloves garlic, minced

¼–½ cup white wine

14 ounces diced tomatoes, fresh or canned

2 cups jasmine rice (uncooked)

4 cups water

STEPS

- In a large saucepan, brown the sausages over medium heat. Remove sausages from the pan, cut them into pieces about the same size as the ribs or perhaps a little smaller, and set aside.
- In the same large saucepan, sauté the onion and red bell pepper in olive oil until they are translucent.
- Season ribs with salt. Add to the saucepan and cook until you don't see pink anymore, about 8 minutes. Add the garlic and cook for just a couple of minutes, stirring to make sure the garlic doesn't burn. Splash in some white wine to deglaze the pan. Stir to help dissolve anything that has stuck to the pan in cooking, returning all those flavors to the food. Add tomatoes.
- Cover and bring to a simmer. Cook on very low heat for 45 minutes.
- Return the sausage to the pan. Mix in the rice and water. Cover and continue cooking on very low heat for 15–20 minutes, until most of the liquid has disappeared and the rice is tender.
- Turn off the heat and let the dish rest for 5 minutes before serving.

Daniel

This recipe calls for pork ribs to be cut in half. Ask your butcher to cut them for you. If you've never spoken to anybody behind the butcher's counter before, this recipe is a great opportunity to establish this very important relationship. Being friends with the butcher will come in handy often.

You could cut the ribs yourself with a meat cleaver, but you run the risk of chipping the bone. Nobody likes bone chips. You could use a meat saw, if you have one. In a pinch, you could even make the dish with whole ribs, but trust me, it's just not the same. Don't be shy – just ask your butcher!

SERVING SUGGESTION

Arugula salad goes great with this meal.

Daniel

Everybody knows what a meatball is. We have meatballs in Spain, too, but the Spanish word for this is "albondigas" (al-BON-de-GAHS) which isn't an exact match because albondigas don't need to be made of meat. For example, albondigas can be made of fish, as they are in this recipe. But "food ball" doesn't sound appealing, and "fish ball" is even worse, so I'll stick with the Spanish name for this dish.

Albondigas de Pescado (Fish Meatballs)

Makes about 18 meatballs

INGREDIENTS

2 eggs

1 teaspoon white vinegar

Olive oil for frying

1 small red pepper

1 medium onion

1 pound pollock

½ teaspoon dry parsley

White pepper and red pepper flakes to taste

Salt to taste

½ cup all-purpose flour

3 garlic cloves

½ cup of white wine

1 (28-ounce) can stewed tomatoes

STEPS

- Soft poach the eggs in water with the white vinegar. Put them in a food processor.
- At this point you can start to gently heat up the olive oil in a frying pan – enough to submerge at least three-fourths of the albondigas.
- Remove the stem and seeds of the red pepper and combine with the eggs in the processor. Add half of the onion to this and blend for a few seconds. Then add the pollock, parsley and pepper flakes. Blend until it becomes a uniform paste. Finish it with a dash of salt and let it chill for 15 minutes in the fridge.
- Form 1–1½-inch albondigas, same as meatballs. Lightly roll in flour.
- Dice up the other half of the onion. In a deep sauté pan sweat the onion (gently cook in oil or water for a few minutes to release the onion's moisture).
- With a mortar and pestle or the food processor, make a paste of the garlic cloves and a pinch of salt. Dilute with the white wine.

- Add the stewed tomatoes to the onions and sauté for a few minutes. Add the garlic and wine mix and simmer the tomato sauce.
- In pan with the olive oil, fry the albondigas until they turn a nice golden brown. Should only take a few minutes. The oil should be hot but not smoking. If it starts to smoke, reduce heat. Flip albondigas in oil to make sure they get evenly browned.
- As they finish frying, transfer them into the tomato sauce. When all the albondigas are in the sauce, cover and let simmer for 15 minutes.

SERVING SUGGESTION

A glass of wine and a little bread is all you need with this dish.

Daniel

This recipe is a great example of trying to match a food memory from my childhood with the ingredients that are available to me now, half a world and thirty years away.

Beans are the foundation of many classic comfort foods in cuisines around the world, and each region has its own familiar varieties that people know and love. Just as cannellini beans are to Tuscany – a staple ingredient of cuisine in the Tuscan region of Italy – faba beans are to the Asturian region of Spain. "Faba" sounds like "fava," so you might think that fava beans (broad beans) would be a good substitute for Asturian faba beans, but they're closer to cannellini beans in texture and flavor.

Chicken and White Bean Stew

Makes 6 servings

INGREDIENTS

1 pound dry great northern beans

2 red bell peppers, divided

1 leek

1 whole chicken, cut into 8 pieces

3 tablespoons olive oil, divided

3 garlic cloves, minced

2 tablespoons parsley, chopped

Salt to taste

1 cup white wine

1 small green pepper

1 onion

1 large carrot

2 bay leaves

STEPS

- Soak the beans overnight for at least 12 hours.
- Preheat the oven to 400°F.
- Clean and rough chop one of the red peppers and the leek.
- Put the chicken in a big oven-safe baking pan or dish. Pour 2 tablespoons of the oil over the chicken and rub it with the garlic, parsley and salt. Add the chopped red pepper and leek to the pan. Pour wine over all the ingredients and use your hands to mix them together. Put the pan in the oven and bake for 45 minutes.
- Pour 2 cups of hot water over the chicken, then allow the pan to cool.
- Remove the chicken and set aside.
- Use an immersion blender to liquefy the remaining vegetables in the pan. Strain the liquid mixture and set aside.

- Discard the water used to soak the beans. In an 8-quart stockpot, cover the beans with fresh cold water and set over high heat.
- Finely dice the remaining red pepper, onion and carrot, and add them to the pot along with the remaining tablespoon of olive oil and the bay leaves. Bring the beans to a boil, then reduce to a simmer.
- Add chicken and blended vegetable stock to the beans. Cover and cook until beans are tender, 45 minutes to an hour. Add salt to taste.

Most supermarkets seem to stock cannellini beans (sometimes labeled "white kidney beans") now, so I'll use those if I can't wait for fabas to be shipped from Spain. (Yes, I actually do this from time to time, and yes, I sometimes plan meals that far in advance!) In recent years, I have enjoyed making this dish with great northern beans. They are probably among the easiest beans to find at the grocery store, so this recipe uses great northern beans.

TIP

The chicken can be made the day before while the beans are soaking.

Cod Fish Cakes

Makes about 12 cod fish cakes

INGREDIENTS

1 pound cod, boned

4–6 potatoes

Salt and pepper to taste

2 tablespoons milk

2 tablespoons chopped fresh parsley (flat leaf)

4 tablespoons grated Romano cheese

4 tablespoons flour

2 eggs

1 cup breadcrumbs

Vegetable oil for frying

STEPS

- Poach the cod gently in simmering water. When it begins to flake you can take it off the heat and allow to cool down. Use your fingers to shred the cod and make sure there are no bones.
- Boil the potatoes, peel and mash. Add the salt and pepper, milk, parsley, cheese, flour and eggs.
- Fold in the shredded cod and form into flattened ball shapes.
- Roll in breadcrumbs and fry in vegetable oil until golden brown on both sides. Drain on paper towels.
- Serve with a mixture of ketchup and horseradish.

Chris

This was a Lenten dish that we asked for year round. A little cod was mixed in with a lot of mashed potatoes, formed into patties and fried to golden brown. Mom thought she was being economical and we thought we were eating like kings and queens.

Daniel

In my opinion food is to be shared. Sharing food creates memories and bonds between friends and family across generations. As the master of a treasured recipe, you have the power not only to connect with the people you feed directly, but also to pass on the recipe itself, empowering more cooks to give life to the recipe, to feed and connect with others in turn.

But not sharing a recipe gives you a certain power, too. Some cooks master recipes and techniques to produce amazing food but keep their secrets. Secret ingredients, secret techniques, secret procedures. This is the power of the dark side. My Aunt Maite holds this power over me.

Aunt Maite has shared other recipes with me – her coconut flan, for example (page 170). But for some reason, her pollo al ajillo (garlic chicken) is different.

Pollo al Ajillo (Garlic Chicken)

Makes 4 servings

INGREDIENTS

4 chicken thighs

4 chicken drums

Salt and pepper to taste

4 cups olive oil, approximately

16 garlic cloves, peeled

1 cup white wine

2 tablespoons chopped fresh parsley

½ lemon

STEPS

- Use paper towels to dab the pieces of chicken to make sure they are very dry. Season the chicken pieces with salt and pepper.
- Pour ¾-inch of olive oil into a frying pan, a sauté pan with high sides, or even a wide pot. Put the garlic cloves in the oil and begin heating over medium heat. Cook until the garlic cloves turn a light golden color all over. Remove the garlic immediately and set aside. (Overcooked garlic that becomes too dark is burnt and will give the oil a bitter flavor.)
- At this point the oil will be ready for the chicken. Gently lay the pieces of chicken in the oil. Don't overcrowd the pan or the cold chicken will make the oil too cold to fry properly. Fry for 8–10 minutes on each side. The chicken's internal temperature should be 165°F.
- Remove the pieces of chicken from the oil and set aside. (You can put the chicken right on the dish you're planning to use for serving so that you don't have to dirty another dish.) Repeat until all the chicken is fried.

- Drain all but ½ cup of oil from the pan. Add the garlic cloves, chicken, wine and parsley. Cover and simmer over medium heat until the liquid is reduced by half.
- Put the chicken back on the serving dish and pour the garlic sauce on top. Squeeze a little lemon juice over the chicken before serving.

She makes it for me when I visit and we have long, vague conversations about it like two spies trying to tease out the other's secrets without giving away too much. "It's simple," she'll say. "Nothing special. Just tell me how you tried making it." So I start to tell her how I tried preparing it most recently based on things I have guessed from the taste of the dish or glimpsed through her swinging kitchen door. "Yes," she says, "That sounds about right." When I ask her questions, her only reply is a noncommittal humming noise, and she gets very busy, bustling around, too "distracted" to make a specific answer. But no matter how I try to reproduce it, her chicken is always better!

This is a good recipe. It's fantastic, actually. But it's still not as good as Maite's chicken.

This dish calls for thighs and drums, but you could also use a fryer chicken cut up into 8 pieces.

Daniel

In the Spanish-speaking world, an "empanada" is a meat pie and "empanadillas" are miniature meat pies shaped into a half moon. Of course, pies like this are popular in other countries and cuisines as well. The fillings change from place to place, but no matter how you fill them they are a perfect portable meal for a journey or a workday lunchbox.

When I was growing up, empanadas appeared for picnics or weekend getaways when there was no time for serious, formal meal preparation. My grandma just put together some filling from whatever was on hand, popped the pies in the oven, and away we went.

In my family, they used to tell a story about one of these road trips: when it was time for lunch, my grandma discovered me napping with my head pillowed on the cloth bag that contained the empanadas! I don't remember that much about it, but I'm sure such a pillow gave me sweet dreams.

Tuna Empanada or Empanadillas

Makes 1 empanada or about 100 empanadillas

DOUGH

INGREDIENTS

1 cup salted butter, room temperature

1 cup water

2½ cups flour

STEPS

- Put the soft butter in the mixer bowl and use the paddle attachment to mix it at medium speed. Slowly pour in the water and mix until all the water is incorporated into the butter.
- Stop the mixer and pour in all the flour. Begin mixing slowly, gradually return to a medium speed, and stop as soon as most of the flour is mixed in. If there's a little flour still left around the edges of the dough, mix it in with a rubber spatula.
- Wrap dough in plastic wrap and refrigerate for at least 2 hours or up to 3 days.

FILLING

INGREDIENTS

12 ounces canned albacore tuna in oil

½ medium onion, finely diced

½ green pepper

1 tablespoon olive oil

1 garlic clove, minced

8 ounces tomato sauce

Salt to taste

STEPS

- Empty the canned tuna into a strainer over a mixing bowl to drain away the oil while you work with the other ingredients.
- In a saucepan over medium heat, sauté the onion and pepper in the olive oil. Add the garlic and cook until translucent. Pour in the tomato sauce and combine.
- With the back of your mixing spoon, gently press down on the tuna in the strainer to remove excess oil. (It doesn't have to be completely dry, just not dripping oil.) Add the tuna to the tomato sauce and cook for 3–4 minutes, constantly stirring to break up the tuna and mix it into the sauce. Let the filling cool.

EGG WASH

INGREDIENT

1 egg

STEPS

- Beat egg in a small bowl and set aside.

(continued)

The dough for these pastries can either be a bread-type dough or a more flaky, buttery dough like a piecrust. This recipe uses the piecrust-type dough and simple tuna filling that was favored in my family.

TIPS

For best results, the dough should be chilled for at least 2 hours. I often make the dough a day before I intend to use it. You can make it 2 or 3 days ahead of time and it will be fine in the fridge. The filling, too, can be made ahead of time and assembled into an empanada when your schedule permits.

If you use a slightly smaller baking dish and have leftover dough and filling, make a few empanadillas and bake them while you bake the empanada.

TO MAKE AN EMPANADA

STEPS

- Preheat oven to 400°F.
- Cut the dough into two equal pieces. Roll out the dough on a floured surface to a ⅛-inch thickness.
- Place the dough in the bottom of a 3-quart casserole dish or 9x13-inch cake pan. Spread filling all over the dough except for a ½-inch border at the edges.
- Roll out the second half of the dough in the same way as the first and lay it on top of the filling. If you want, you can trim off some of the excess dough at this point (later you can use the extra dough to decorate the top crust).
- Pinch and fold the top and bottom layers of dough together all the way around, sealing in the filling. If you choose to decorate the top crust, use the dough trimmings to create lines, a grid, or other design.
- Dip a pastry brush into the bowl with the beaten egg and coat the whole surface of the empanada with egg.
- Use a fork to poke small holes in the surface of the dough at regular intervals so that hot air can escape as the empanada bakes. Bake for 35 minutes.

TO MAKE EMPANADILLAS

STEPS

- Preheat oven to 400°F.
- Roll out the dough to about ⅛-inch thick.
- Use a biscuit cutter or cookie cutter to make dough circles about 2¾ inches in diameter.
- Place filling on one half of the circle. (If you have never made an empanadilla or dumpling before, use just a little less filling than you think you need. Too much filling makes it hard to seal the dough at the edges.)
- Flip the other side of the circle over to cover the filling. Press the tines of a fork gently all around the semicircular edge of the dough to seal it and keep the filling inside while it bakes.
- Dip a pastry brush into the bowl with the beaten egg and coat the surface of each empanadilla with egg.
- Poke each empanadilla once with the tines of a fork so that hot air can escape during baking. Space the empanadillas evenly on a baking sheet and bake for 12 minutes.

Daniel

Culinary training teaches you to avoid waste as a business practice, particularly with expensive ingredients like meat. It's true that meat is expensive, but most chefs I know also avoid wasting meat out of a sense of respect and obligation to the creatures that were slaughtered for food. Restaurant patrons may turn up their noses at dishes made from the less common parts of the animal, but if chefs could follow their own preferences, many of them would be adding things like liver, tripe and tongue to the menu.

Tongue was a delicacy in our grandparents' time, and it still is a delicacy for those who know good food. It requires a little extra preparation but the result is worth it: a piece of meat as large and tender as a beef tenderloin, with the flavor and texture of the best short ribs you've ever had.

This recipe works very well in a pressure cooker, but if you don't have one then a stock pot will do. This slow-cooking dish can be made in a sauté pan as described here or cooked slowly in a crock pot for a few hours. I like to make tongue the day before I plan to serve it and then heat it the next day while I'm making the side dishes.

Tongue

Makes 4 servings

INGREDIENTS

1 beef tongue

Salt and black pepper to taste

2 carrots, divided

1 large onion

2 bay leaves

5 garlic cloves, divided

A few whole black peppercorns

1 sprig rosemary

1 sprig thyme

3 tablespoons olive oil, divided

1 tablespoon all-purpose flour

3 tablespoons tomato sauce

1 cup white wine

¼ teaspoon oregano

STEPS

- Wash the beef tongue in cold water. Season it with salt and pepper and put it in a pressure cooker or regular stock pot. Add 1 whole carrot, half of the onion, the bay leaves, 2 of the garlic cloves, black peppercorns, and sprigs of rosemary and thyme. Cover the ingredients with water and bring to a boil. Simmer for 20 minutes in the pressure cooker or 1 hour in the stock pot.
- Remove the pot from heat. Use tongs to remove the tongue from the pot and set it aside to cool. Conserve the stock; it will be used to make gravy.
- When the tongue is cool enough to handle, use a paring knife to peel away the hard outer white skin from the meat. Cut the beef into ¼-inch slices.
- In a large sauté pan, heat 2 tablespoons of the olive oil over medium heat. Brown the beef on both sides in the oil, then remove from the oil and set aside.

- Finely dice the other half of the onion and sauté it in the same oil in the same pan for about 5 minutes. You may need to add another tablespoon of olive oil if you notice the onions looking a little dry. Meanwhile, dice the remaining carrot and mince the remaining garlic. As the onion starts to get golden brown, add the carrot and garlic and cook them over medium heat for another 10 minutes.
- Sprinkle flour over the vegetables in the pan and stir. Stir in the tomato sauce and wine and cook for another 5 minutes. Pour 2 cups of the stock through a strainer into the sauté pan. Add the oregano.
- Arrange the beef in the sauté pan, making sure all the meat is covered with stock. Add more stock if necessary, again pouring the stock through a strainer into the sauté pan. Simmer for an hour and test to see if the beef is tender. If not, keep cooking until the beef is tender. Remove from the pan and set aside.
- Use an immersion blender to liquefy the vegetables in the sauté pan and return the beef to the pan. Add a little more salt and pepper to taste.

SERVING SUGGESTION

Serve hot with potatoes (roasted, mashed or fried) and veggies for a hearty homestyle meal.

Meatloaf

Makes 8 servings

INGREDIENTS

2 pounds ground beef

1 egg

1 cup cooked rice

1 cup milk

1 tablespoon Worcestershire sauce

1 onion, grated

1½ teaspoons salt

½ teaspoon pepper

¼ cup ketchup

4 slices bacon

STEPS

- Preheat the oven to 350°F.
- Mix the ground beef with the egg, rice, milk, Worcestershire, onion, salt and pepper.
- Put into a 9x5-inch loaf pan and push down to remove any air pockets. Spread the ketchup on top of the loaf.
- Cut the bacon strips in half crosswise and lay the stips across the meatloaf. Bake until the bacon is crisp and a thermometer registers at least 170°F.
- Let the meatloaf rest for a few minutes before cutting and serving.
- I'm sure you know that this makes the most delicious sandwiches for the next day, hot or cold.

Chris

I'm not sure of the origins of this all-American comfort food but it certainly was a favorite of Depression-era housewives. By the time I was growing up in the 1950s you couldn't find a women's magazine on a rack at the supermarket that didn't feature some new way to spruce up this old standby. Chopped meat was less expensive than steak and it could be augmented with fillers such as breadcrumbs or rice that stretched it even further. It is the beef that I grew up with and this is the meatloaf version I remember.

Chris

If there was a comfort food hall of fame, mashed potatoes would be at the very top of the list, edging out macaroni and cheese by a noodle. It is a dish with very few moving parts, consisting basically of potatoes, butter, cream or milk, salt and pepper. But perfectly fluffy, creamy smooth mashed potatoes can be an elusive goal. What kind of potatoes are best? Should they be boiled skins on or skins off? Do you use a potato masher, hand mixer or wire whisk? Over time, cooks develop their own personal preferences. Here is a version that uses very traditional techniques to create one of the simplest of pleasures.

Mashed Potatoes

Makes 6 servings

INGREDIENTS

3 pounds russet or white potatoes

1 cup milk

1 stick butter

Salt and pepper to taste

STEPS

- Scrub but do not peel the potatoes and place in a saucepan with enough water to cover. Bring the water to a boil and then reduce to a simmer. Cook slowly until the potatoes are tender and a fork goes in and out easily. Drain in a colander.
- Heat the milk in a small saucepan and add the butter. Stir until melted.
- Peel the potatoes while still warm and put them through a ricer into their original pot. Add the warm milk and butter and mix with the riced potatoes using a whisk. Add salt and pepper to taste.

Chris

Over the years, I've been asked to judge at dozens of different chili contests. And that's fun because I'm a real chili lover and the varieties of recipes and inventiveness of the cooks are always an inspiration. There are chilies that have 40–50 ingredients, complicated spice mixes, three-day preparations, special cooking utensils, and so on. But the chili that always comes to my mind when I want to enjoy it as a simple pleasure is the mock chili that my mother made as a way of using a little chopped meat to feed a lot of people. After many years of just remembering how much we loved this dish, I finally decided to make a batch for myself. It was just as delicious and satisfying as I remembered.

All-American Chili

Makes 4 servings

INGREDIENTS

1 pound chopped meat

1 onion

1 can Campbell's Pork and Beans

STEPS

- Crumble and fry the beef in a skillet until all the moisture has been released and the meat begins to brown. Stir in the onions and cook until the onions are soft. Add the can of beans and stir well.
- Let simmer for 15–20 minutes until everything is bubbling.

EAT YOUR VEGGIES

Chris – My grandmother had us convinced that eggplant was "the other dark meat." Vegetables were the stars in her cooking show and meats were bit players. For one thing, meats were more expensive in those days. And pound for pound they still are. With vegetables you can be extravagant, and a giant baking dish mounded high with eggplant parmigiana is a pretty impressive sight on the dinner table. Vegetables feed the creative spirit of the cook with endless variations of cooking methods, combinations, flavoring, colors and textures. And when all is said and done, there is nothing more elemental, more of a simple pleasure, than the taste of the things that grow out of the good earth.

Daniel – I grew up in Europe, where farmers markets were just "markets" – a commonplace and expected part of everyday life. I trailed behind my grandmother on her many trips to the market, watching how she chose the vegetables for our meals, but I didn't have much interest in this activity until I saw fruits and vegetables actually growing. In the summers, we kids were lucky enough to spend time living in a small village, where everybody had at least a household garden, if not several fields of crops. Sometimes we stayed with my Aunt Mina and Uncle Zoilo, who had a farm and roadside restaurant. Their plot of land was small, steep, and divided by a minor highway, but every possible meter was cultivated, and yielded greens, figs, cherries, potatoes, beans, even kiwis! Zoilo put us to work. There, I saw plants sprouting from the dirt, growing and flowering, every stalk, branch and vine bursting with the stuff that ended up on display in the market stalls. Suddenly, shopping and even eating produce was much more interesting. To this day, I love to supply my kitchen with food from my own garden. No other fruit or vegetable will taste as good as the one you grow yourself.

Chris

As part of our Sunday antipasto, my grandmother would often prepare some sautéed mushrooms, seasoned with oil and vinegar and served room temperature. This variation uses the meaty baby portabella mushrooms and the rich flavor of Marsala wine.

Mushrooms Marsala

Makes 6 servings

INGREDIENTS

2 pounds baby bella mushrooms

3 tablespoons olive oil

¼ cup Marsala wine

Salt and pepper to taste

Fresh parsley, chopped

STEPS

- Clean the mushrooms with a damp paper towel and trim the stems. Cut into halves, or quarters if the mushrooms are more than an inch in diameter.
- Heat the oil in a skillet and sauté the mushrooms over medium-high heat, stirring frequently until they give up their moisture and begin to brown. Add the wine and continue to cook until the wine is almost completely evaporated.
- Season with salt and fresh pepper and sprinkle with freshly chopped parsley.

Fava Beans

Makes 5–6 cups

INGREDIENTS

2 cups dried fava beans

1 tablespoon olive oil

1 clove garlic, minced

1 teaspoon oregano

1 teaspoon salt

STEPS

- Rinse the beans and cover them with water. Let them sit overnight.
- Drain the beans and put them in a pot with water to cover and add the remaining ingredients. Bring to a boil, then lower to a simmer.
- Cook for 2 hours or until the beans are soft and the skins slip off easily. Be patient. They take a long time to get soft.
- I like to enjoy these beans lukewarm as a snack, but I guess you could shell them and serve as a side dish.

Chris

Until they are soaked and boiled, dry fava beans look like gravel stones from the driveway. But when they are softened they slip right out of their skins, infused with the flavors of garlic and oregano and dressed with a little olive oil and balsamico.

NOTE

The conventional wisdom about cooking beans is not to add salt to the cooking water or the beans will never get tender. I have no idea where that idea came from. It has no basis in chemistry or cooking that I know.

Chris

The only time to make and enjoy this dish is in the summer when tomatoes are at their juicy perfection. Adding salt to the cut-up tomatoes forces them to give up their juices and create a savory dressing infused with the flavor of oregano. Gram would make a bowl of these and leave them on the counter to macerate. We would sneak into the bowl with a piece of bread to soak up some of the juice. Later, Gram would come back to the kitchen and remark, "The tomatoes aren't as juicy this year." Oh, yes they were, Gram!

Tomatoes Oreganata

Makes 4 servings

INGREDIENTS

4 tomatoes

2 tablespoons olive oil

1 teaspoon oregano

1 teaspoon salt

Pepper to taste

STEPS

- Cut the tomatoes into 1-inch cubes. Put them in a bowl with the olive oil, oregano, salt and pepper.
- Toss well and let sit, covered, on the counter for at least an hour.
- The longer they sit, the more juice will be created. Serve with lots of bread to soak up the juice.

Carrots with Thyme

Makes 6 servings

INGREDIENTS

8–10 carrots (purple, orange, yellow)

¼ teaspoon fresh thyme

¼ teaspoon Dijon mustard

1 teaspoon honey

½ tablespoon olive oil

Salt and pepper to taste

STEPS

- Peel carrots and cut ½-inch slices at an angle.
- In a saucepan, cover the sliced carrots with water. Add the thyme and a pinch of salt. Cover and cook until soft. Drain the water. Gently stir in the olive oil, honey and mustard.
- Add salt and black pepper to taste.

Daniel

Carrots can get overlooked, but I love them. I grow them in my garden and I use them often. When trying to enhance the natural flavors of garden produce, whether they are leafy greens, root vegetables, beans, fruits or vegetables, you usually need just a few staple ingredients, workhorses of the kitchen, to make them shine. This is why I always have honey, thyme and Dijon available in my kitchen.

TIP

You can give this simple side dish some added visual interest by combining carrots of different colors.

Chris

Flour-egg-bread, flour-egg-bread. These three steps were some of my first kitchen chores to help in the preparation of chicken, pork or veal cutlets – and the ingredient we called the "other dark meat": eggplant. The coating process keeps all the flavors and moisture inside while providing a nice crunchy exterior.

TIP

Look for eggplants that are shiny, dark and smooth with no wrinkles or blemishes. It helps if the stems are bright green.

Eggplant Parmigiana

Makes 8 servings

INGREDIENTS

2 large eggplants

3 eggs, beaten

1 cup flour

1 cup Italian breadcrumbs

½ cup olive oil

2 cups ricotta

1 tablespoon chopped parsley

Salt and pepper

1 quart spaghetti sauce

½ pound sliced or grated mozzarella cheese

1 cup grated Parmigiano Reggiano cheese

Oil

STEPS

- Peel eggplants in stripes lengthwise. Cut crosswise in ⅓-inch slices. Sprinkle with salt and let sit in a colander for 10 minutes to remove excess moisture. Rinse the slices and pat dry.
- Coat each slice lightly in flour, then dip in egg, then in crumbs. Fry in oil until golden brown on both sides. Drain fried slices on paper towels.
- Preheat the oven to 350°F.
- Coat bottom of a 9x13-inch baking dish with spaghetti sauce.
- Mix the ricotta with the chopped parsley and a little salt and pepper.
- Layer pan with fried eggplant, sauce, ricotta, mozzarella and Parmigiano cheeses. Top the final layer of eggplant with sauce, mozzarella and Parmigiano. Cover with foil and bake for 45 minutes to an hour.
- Remove from oven. Let stand for 15 minutes. Serve with more sauce.

Daniel

In general, the less you do to mushrooms, the better they are. That's a good reason for a chef to like mushrooms, but I've actually been fascinated by them since I was little. I like how they pop up so magically overnight; how they can be concealed all around you in a forest or meadow – until you know the secrets of where and when they like to grow; how they show so much variation in shape, size and color, yet sometimes display only slight differences between edible and inedible varieties. Every year I learn more about mushrooms and my appreciation grows stronger.

Other than the common white mushrooms, oyster mushrooms were among the first fresh mushrooms I ever cooked. To this day I still love the aroma and sound of them searing as they hit a hot skillet.

Setas a la Plancha (Sautéed Mushrooms)

Makes 2 servings

INGREDIENTS

2 cups oyster mushrooms

1 tablespoon olive oil

1 garlic clove, minced

1 tablespoon finely chopped parsley

Salt

STEPS

- Heat a griddle or cast iron pan over medium-high heat.
- While the griddle heats, trim the ends of the oyster mushrooms. Dust off any visible dirt. Separate joined mushrooms into single-stemmed pieces. Put the mushrooms in a mixing bowl with garlic and parsley. Add the olive oil and toss the ingredients gently. Add a pinch of salt.
- Test the griddle with a few drops of water to see if it's reached the correct temperature: hot enough that droplets of water will ball up and roll across the surface, but not so hot that water droplets sizzle instantly to nothing.
- When the griddle is heated lay the mushrooms on the griddle to cook for a couple of minutes. They'll be ready to turn when they come off the hot surface easily with the help of a spatula. Avoid poking and turning them too much; you don't want them to break up. If they look a little dry after they're done, you can drizzle a little more olive oil on top.
- Serve fresh off the griddle.

Daniel

Fresh tomatoes are one of the great joys of summer. My favorite way to eat them is sliced and drizzled with a little olive oil, and sometimes sprinkled with salt. This recipe is another simple approach that makes the most of the fresh tomato flavor. If you are serving guests, a preparation like this has an advantage over tossed salad because you can see the number of portions at a glance.

Guacamole Stuffed Tomatoes

Makes 8 servings

INGREDIENTS

8 Kumato tomatoes

2 avocados

1 jalapeño, minced

1 green onion, minced

1 garlic clove

1 lime

½ cup chopped cilantro

1 cup shredded queso fresco

STEPS

- Set a mesh strainer inside a mixing bowl.
- Place tomatoes on a cutting board and slice off the tops (about ¼ inch down). Remove and discard the stem from each tomato top, dice the tops, and put the diced tops into the mesh strainer.
- Scoop the flesh out of all the tomatoes, dice the flesh, and add it to the strainer. Mince the garlic clove, jalapeño and green onion, and add to the diced tomatoes in the strainer.
- Slice the avocados in half and remove the pits. Scoop the avocado flesh onto the cutting board, dice it into ½-inch chunks, and add it to the strainer.
- Slice the lime in half. Hold each half above the tomato-and-avocado mixture as you squeeze the juice over the mixture. Let the extra lime juice and tomato water drain into the bowl. You want to keep the mixture in the strainer as dry as possible. See Tip on the following page for ways to use the reserved juice.

- Add the cilantro and mix all the ingredients together gently so that the pieces of avocado hold their shape.
- Stuff the hollowed-out tomatoes generously with the tomato-and-avocado mixture. Sprinkle with queso fresco before serving.

TIP

Reserve the juice drained from limes and tomatoes for use in an agua fresca-style drink or a Bloody Mary.

Daniel

If you are lucky enough to have an Italian deli or grocery in your neighborhood, you may have enjoyed the aroma of red peppers frying in olive oil. I love the smell of peppers cooking, whether they're being charred over an open flame, frying in a pan, or baking in the oven as we'll do in this recipe.

These roasted peppers are served as a "tapa" – what you might call a "small plate" or appetizer – on a slice of fresh or toasted bread, but I can make a meal of them served alongside anchovies, sardines or Serrano ham. Try it and see if you agree!

Piperrada (Roasted Peppers)

Makes 10 servings

INGREDIENTS

1 sweet or yellow onion

4 cloves garlic, unpeeled

2 red bell peppers

2 yellow bell peppers

2 poblano peppers

1 tablespoon whole cumin seed

2 tablespoons olive oil

Salt

STEPS

- Preheat the oven to 450°F.
- Peel the onion and cut it in half. Put it on a sheet pan or cookie tray along with the unpeeled garlic and peppers.
- Pour olive oil over the peppers, onions, and garlic, and sprinkle them with cumin seeds and salt. Use tongs to toss all these ingredients together until everything is coated in oil.
- Put the sheet pan in the oven and bake for 20 minutes. At the 10-minute mark, flip the peppers and onion over so that they cook evenly and continue baking for the remaining 10 minutes.
- Put all the vegetables in a mixing bowl to cool. Cover the bowl to let the peppers "sweat," as this will make them easier to peel.
- When the vegetables have cooled, begin cutting up the peppers:
- Make the first cut while holding the pepper over the mixing bowl in order to preserve as much of the veggie juice as possible. When the juices have drained from the pepper, move to a cutting board.

- Remove the top of the pepper, cut it in half, remove the seeds, and flip it over to peel off the skin. Cut the pepper into strips and put the strips into another mixing bowl. Repeat this process with all the peppers.
- Cut the onion into long, thin wedges and add to the peppers. Cut off the ends of the garlic cloves, squeeze the roasted garlic out onto the cutting board, mince it, and add to the peppers and onions.
- Now pour all the vegetable juice from the first mixing bowl over the peppers, onions and garlic. The juice may be poured through a strainer to remove cumin seeds if desired (I prefer to keep them in the mixture). Gently stir to combine and add salt to taste.

SERVING SUGGESTION

Spoon over slices of fresh or toasted bread accompanied by anchovies, sardines or Serrano ham.

Green Beans with Tomatoes

Makes 8 servings

INGREDIENTS

2 pounds fresh green beans, ends trimmed

1 teaspoon olive oil

1 small can tomato sauce

Salt and pepper to taste

STEPS

- Wash and trim the green beans and run them through the peeler (or simply slice them lengthwise with a knife.
- Heat the oil in a large covered sauté pan and toss the beans to coat with oil for a few minutes. Add the sauce and mix well.
- Cover and cook for 5–10 minutes on low-medium heat. Add salt and pepper to taste.

Chris

I have talked about the various kitchen helper jobs I used to perform in my grandmother's kitchen as she prepared for the weekly Sunday dinner feast. There was always an antipasto with celery salad and olives, mushrooms, cheeses and sliced meats. Then came the pasta with tomato sauce, meatballs and spare ribs. Once that was all cleared away, she rolled in the roast chickens or roast eye round of beef along with some form of potatoes and several green vegetables. My favorite version of the latter was a very simple sauté of green beans in tomato sauce. At the end of our potato peeler was an attachment that would slice the green beans into thin slivers. And so, one by one I fed the green beans through the slots in the handle to "French" them. I don't know if this really made a difference in the flavor of the dish, but it gave me something to do.

Chris

Every season has its own set of special flavors and pleasures. In winter we can warm up to a big bowl of soup or stew, and in summer we get to revel in the fresh flavors from the garden. Today, our markets seem to carry all ingredients all year long. But in the case of tomatoes, I really like to wait until at least mid-summer to take advantage of the outstanding flavor and texture of ripe, locally-grown tomatoes.

Stuffed Tomatoes

Makes 8 servings

INGREDIENTS

8 medium-to-large tomatoes

Salt

1 onion, finely chopped

½ cup olive oil

2–3 anchovies

2 tablespoons parsley

1 tablespoon capers

1 cup breadcrumbs

Pepper

STEPS

- Preheat the oven to 400°F.
- Dip tomatoes into boiling water for one minute, then remove skins. Cut tops off (set these aside), remove seeds and sprinkle insides with salt. Turn over and drain on paper towels.
- Fry the onion in ¼ cup of the olive oil until browned. Remove from the heat and stir in anchovies, parsley, capers and 2 tablespoons of the breadcrumbs with a little pepper.
- Fill tomatoes with the mixture, top with reserved lids and place in an oiled 9x13-inch pan or similar.
- Heat the remaining oil and fry remaining breadcrumbs, stirring until brown. Pour over the tomatoes in pan.
- Cook covered for 30 minutes.

Daniel

Leeks have always intrigued me. As a young kitchen apprentice, I watched the more seasoned cooks gather around a plate of boiled leeks, eating the leeks plain or with a few drops of Tabasco, as if it were some heavenly treat. Of course, when I showed interest they quickly told me that I wouldn't enjoy such things. Eventually, they invited me to try one, and I've been hooked on leeks ever since. I always have a bed of leeks in my garden.

This leek dish is a little more elaborate than a dash of Tabasco, but still simple enough to showcase the main ingredient. It is elegant yet hearty, like a classic gratin.

Leeks in Béchamel

Makes 5 servings

INGREDIENTS

3 leeks, cleaned and cut into 3-inch pieces

1 tablespoon salt, approximately, plus more to taste

3 tablespoons butter

3 tablespoons flour

2 cups milk

¼ teaspoon nutmeg

Pepper to taste

½ cup Parmigiano Reggiano cheese

6–8 slices Serrano ham or prosciutto, sliced thin

STEPS

- Choose a pot large enough to fit all the leeks. Add water to the pot, enough that the leeks will be covered when you add them later. Add about a tablespoon of salt and set the water over medium-high heat.
- When the water boils, gently add the leeks to the pot and boil for about 20 minutes, or until soft when tested with the point of a knife.
- While the leeks are boiling, begin to prepare a béchamel sauce, sometimes called "white sauce." (See steps below.)
- Put the butter in a sauté pan over medium heat. When the butter is melted, stir in the flour and a pinch of salt. Cook the flour mixture for a few minutes, whisking frequently. Slowly pour the milk a little at a time into the hot flour mixture, whisking continually. Wait until each addition of milk is fully mixed in before adding more. Too much cold milk all at once will lead to a lumpy sauce!
- When the milk is all incorporated, reduce heat and cook a little more to thicken. When the sauce looks like it has reached a good, creamy consistency, add nutmeg, pepper, and more salt to taste. Remove the pan from the heat.

TO ASSEMBLE

- When the leeks are done cooking, drain them and set them on a towel to dry. Wrap each section of leek with a slice of Serrano ham and lay the wrapped slices, side by side, down the center of a shallow baking dish.
- Pour the béchamel sauce over the wrapped leeks. Sprinkle with Parmigiano cheese and put under a broiler until the cheese-sprinkled sauce gets a little golden color.

TIP

Leeks grow in sandy soil, so little bits of grit can work themselves into each fold and layer of the leeks. To avoid a gritty mouthful, rinse the leeks several times.

Cucumber and Apple Salad

Makes 6 servings

INGREDIENTS

1 Honeycrisp apple

1 seedless cucumber

1 tablespoon olive oil

2 tablespoons golden balsamic vinegar

¼ cup pumpkin seeds

Salt and ground pink peppercorns to taste

2 tablespoons Stilton cheese, crumbled

Zest of ½ lemon

STEPS

- Core the apple, cut into wedges, and put the slices in a mixing bowl. Cut the cucumber in angled slices about the same thickness as the apple wedges and add them to the mixing bowl.
- Over the apple and cucumber slices pour olive oil, vinegar, pumpkin seeds, a pinch of salt, and ground pink peppercorns – just a few twists of the pepper grinder.
- Toss ingredients together until well coated with vinegar and oil.
- Place the mixture in a serving dish. Serve topped with crumbled cheese and sprinkled with lemon zest.

Daniel

I love apples, so it's no surprise to find apples appearing at my table as part of any meal, whether breakfast, lunch or dinner. Apples can be a great addition to vegetable dishes and – as you'll soon find out if you try this recipe – apples love cucumbers.

VARIATIONS

This is a recipe that can easily accommodate seasonal changes of ingredients. The apples, cucumbers, soft cheese, vinegar and oil remain the same, but the pumpkin seeds can be replaced by pomegranate seeds, slices of kumquat, pine nuts, or even black sesame seeds as your pantry permits. Fresh mint is a great addition in the summertime.

The recipe calls for you to season the salad by grinding pink peppercorns on top, but if you don't have pink peppercorns then black ones will be fine. Likewise, the Stilton cheese can be replaced by a similar cheese like a dry, creamy ricotta.

SWEETS FOR THE SWEET

Chris – When I look back on my childhood, I realize that Mom always had something sweet for dessert. Maybe it was just be a cup of pudding or Jell-O or a scoop of ice cream, but often it was something homemade to top off the evening meal. It might be a piece of pie or a baked apple or a simple cookie. We usually waited until the dishes were washed, dried and put away and then we sat back at the table. The whole ritual added to the excitement and enjoyment of even the simplest of desserts.

Daniel – My childhood was much different from Chris's when it came to sweets. Only a few special desserts were made at home. The region of Asturias is famed for its pastries. In Oviedo there is a pastry shop on every corner, each renowned for its own specialty. It is common to buy a tray of assorted pastries from one of these shops for special events or get-togethers. My culinary training unlocked many of the mysteries of these familiar desserts and my travels introduced me to even more kinds of desserts than I could have imagined as a kid. As an adult, I enjoy using this knowledge to recreate the delicacies I miss from my hometown and my travels.

Chris

Some simple pleasures from the kitchen come with hidden benefits. When the leaves start to turn in the fall and the temperatures dip below freezing at night, the markets are filled with a new crop of apples. Now is the time to enjoy them at their freshest and most flavorful. Pick a variety that cooks well, like Empire, Rome Beauties, Jonathans, Jonagolds, Honey Crisps, etc. As they slowly bake in the oven, your house will fill with the aromas of cinnamon, apple and nutmeg. This is also a great recipe to make with young children since the prep is simple and the final product is bound to please.

Baked Apples

Makes 4 servings

INGREDIENTS

4 Rome Beauty apples

4 tablespoons butter, softened

4 tablespoons brown sugar

1 teaspoon cinnamon

Nutmeg

STEPS

- Preheat the oven to 350°F.
- Core the apples, leaving about ½ inch at the bottom of each to hold the liquid.
- Combine the softened butter with the brown sugar, cinnamon and a few gratings of nutmeg.
- Place the apples in a baking dish and fill each with the butter/sugar mixture. Bake for 40 minutes or until the apples are tender.
- Spoon the sauce that has gathered in the pan back over the apples and cool before serving.

Applesauce

Makes 4–6 cups

INGREDIENTS

6–8 apples (MacIntosh, Gala, Empire, etc.)

¼ cup brown sugar

¼ cup white sugar

1 cinnamon stick

1 cup water

STEPS

- Quarter the apples and place them in a saucepan with the sugar, cinnamon stick and water. Bring to a boil and then lower to a simmer. Cook for 20–30 minutes until the apples are completely soft.
- Remove the cinnamon stick and let cool for a few minutes before passing through a foley food mill to remove the skin and pits.

Chris

My mom was the original Frugal Gourmet. She never let anything go to waste. Chicken bones, necks and feet became chicken stock for soups and gravies. If vegetables got soft in the refrigerator they were added to soups and stews. And apples that started to bruise or shrivel were bound for applesauce. There were some meals that were naturals for a side dish of applesauce, like pork chops or fritters. Other times we just enjoyed it as a light dessert or TV snack.

NOTE

Cooking with the skins adds more nutrients and color to the sauce but if you don't have a food mill you can simply peel and core the apples before cooking.

Daniel

I think even before I was interested in cooking I was interested in ice cream. (What child isn't?) I probably took it a little further than most kids, though. I remember freezing fruit at a very early age and being completely fascinated with the change of texture and flavor. I discovered sorbet as I was cutting frozen grapes and the frozen grape shavings piled up on my cutting board. That was the start of many experiments with granita and sorbet-like frozen concoctions. Some I remember as being pretty good…others, not so much. Looking back, I can't believe that my grandmother let me play with the freezer as much as I did.

This recipe calls for you to hollow out the orange, scraping the fruit out through a hole in the top so that the emptied peel can be used as a bowl for the ice cream – a rustic yet elegant way to serve this dessert. After being scraped out of the peel, the fruit is liquefied with an immersion blender and strained through a colander. This method gives you juice of a thicker consistency that works great for the ice cream. If that sounds too intense, however, you can certainly use an old-fashioned juicer and plain old ice cream bowls. The important thing is to make ice cream and eat ice cream.

Orange Ice Cream

Makes 4–6 cups

INGREDIENTS

6 oranges (Cara Cara oranges are a favorite of mine)

3 cups heavy cream

1½ cups juice

1 cup sugar

2 tablespoons orange zest

2 tablespoons orange liquor (optional)

Red and yellow food coloring (optional)

Mint for garnish

STEPS

- Cut off the top of the oranges to make a hole in the peel. Scrape the fruit out through this hole into a mixing bowl, leaving the peel intact.
- Use an immersion blender to liquefy the fruit, then place the resulting pulpy liquid into a colander over another mixing bowl to remove fibrous bits and seeds. Set liquid aside to strain.
- In the bowl of a mixer, whip the cream at high speed until stiff. Turn the mixer to a lower speed and gradually add orange juice, sugar and zest, as well as liquor if desired, until these ingredients are fully incorporated. (At this point you may intensify the color of the ice cream if you choose by adding red and yellow food coloring, just a drop at a time, until you are satisfied with the color.)
- Put the ice cream in a freezer-safe container and freeze until hard. Do the same with the hollowed-out orange peels. They are easier to work with when they are frozen.
- To serve, scoop the ice cream from the container and fill the oranges as you would fill an ice cream cone. Garnish with a sprig of mint.

Daniel

Flan, a sweet egg custard, is one of the most iconic Spanish desserts. Of course there are many versions, but my family always ate coconut flan. It was my Aunt Maite's signature dessert and we couldn't wait to have it every time we had a meal at her house.

As it bakes, this flan performs a magician's trick: the shredded coconut that you mixed with the other ingredients will rise mysteriously to the top. When you invert the flan for serving, those coconut shreds become a nutty, chewy crust – a great counterpoint for the creamy texture of the flan.

You begin by making caramel, which is used to coat a cake pan. Then you make the flan and pour it into the prepared cake pan. When you bake it, you set the cake pan inside a larger pan, fill the larger pan with water, and bake the flan in its water bath for about an hour.

It doesn't take much time to prepare flan, but you can't make it at the last minute. It takes an hour to bake, a half hour to cool on the counter, and another 2 hours to chill in the refrigerator.

Coconut Flan

Makes 8–10 servings

CARAMEL (prepare this first)

INGREDIENTS

1 cup sugar

¼ cup water

STEPS

- In a small saucepan, mix the sugar with the water. Bring to a boil over high heat. Stir briefly and reduce the heat to medium. Cook about 5 minutes or until the syrup turns a caramel color.
- Immediately pour the caramel into a 9-inch cake pan, tilting and turning the pan to coat its base and sides with caramel. Work fast – the caramel will harden quickly as it cools.
- Place the cake pan in a large casserole dish or roasting pan and set aside.

FLAN

INGREDIENTS

5 eggs

2 egg yolks

1 14-ounce can sweetened condensed milk

1 13.5-ounce can coconut milk

1 cup unsweetened shredded coconut

1/3 cup heavy cream

1 teaspoon vanilla extract

STEPS

- Preheat the oven to 350°F.
- To prepare a hot water bath for the flan, heat a teakettle full of water or run your tap water until it is nice and hot.
- In a medium bowl, using an electric mixer or the whisk attachment of an immersion blender, mix the eggs and egg yolks for 2–3 minutes. Add and mix for another minute: the condensed milk, coconut milk, cream, shredded coconut and vanilla.
- Carefully pour the mixture into the caramelized cake pan that is ready and waiting, sitting in the roasting pan. Set the roasting pan in the oven with the cake pan still inside it. Now gently pour hot water into the roasting pan around the cake pan, until the water comes halfway up the outside of the cake pan.
- Bake for 1 hour or until a knife inserted in the center of the flan comes out clean. Remove the cake pan from the roasting pan. Cool for at least 30 minutes, then cover and refrigerate for at least 2 hours.
- To serve, carefully run a knife around the edge of the cake pan. Cover the cake pan with a serving plate and flip it over. Slowly and gently lift the cake pan, allowing the caramel to run down over the sides of the custard.
- Slice it like a pie, in wedges. Garnish with flaked coconut if desired.

Daniel

Many recipes in this book are inspired by the Spanish foods I grew up with, but this dessert is as American as it gets. Though pie is not part of the Spanish tradition, it was one of the features of my adopted country's home cooking that I enjoyed most as a newcomer.

Apple pie in particular is dear to my heart, not only because it's an American classic but because I am something of an apple nerd. In the north of Spain, we love our apples. Asturias, the region where I'm from, is famous for hard apple cider. My front yard here in the States is a mini-orchard of heritage apple varieties, including Lodi apples, which are the ones I prefer to use in this pie. If you can't find Lodi apples, choose a variety like Granny Smith that's a good baking apple (one that will hold its shape and texture when baked).

For the best crust, I recommend using a combination of butter and lard for shortening. Many American home cooks have never used lard. It was commonly used generations ago, but seems to have been almost completely replaced with vegetable shortening in American recipes because people thought it was healthier. I do not agree, and I do not use vegetable shortening in my own cooking and baking.

Apple Pie

Makes one pie or 8 servings

CRUST

INGREDIENTS

2½ cups flour

1 teaspoon salt

½ cup (1 stick) butter

½ cup lard

¼–½ cup ice water

STEPS

- In a mixing bowl, whisk together flour and salt.
- Remove the butter and lard from the refrigerator. Cut the butter into small pieces and add butter and lard to the flour mixture. With a pastry blender, mix the butter and lard into the flour until it is thoroughly combined, turning a uniform butter-yellow color, with the biggest lumps of shortening no bigger than a pea.
- Sprinkle ice water sparingly onto this mixture, 1/8-cup at a time, stirring gently with a fork or your fingers until the mixture clings together as a dough.
- Divide the dough into 2 portions: 1/3 of the dough will form the top crust, and the remaining 2/3 will form the bottom crust. Roll out the dough immediately or wrap each portion separately in plastic wrap and keep it in the refrigerator while you make the filling.
- Roll out the dough into a circle 12 inches in diameter. Use the rolling pin to help you pick up the dough without tearing it: set the rolling pin at one edge; use your fingers to pick up the edge of the dough and hold it gently against the rolling pin; and then roll and lift the rolling pin away from that edge, turning the rolling pin to draw the pastry over the rolling pin while lifting the rolling pin away from the countertop. When the dough is draped over the rolling pin, quickly lay the dough down gently over a deep-dish pie pan and smooth it gently down to cover the inside of the pan.

(continued)

I am glad to see lard making a comeback. Lard is a staple of European, Central American and South American baking, so if you have trouble finding it in your grocery store, try looking in a local Latin American market. Lard is worth looking for. Pie crust made with lard has an almost elastic quality as you roll it out and makes a reliably tender, flaky pastry. If you have ever been disappointed with pie crust that is fragile when raw or tough when baked, you will be delighted with the difference that lard makes.

VARIATION

If you are sharing your pie with vegetarians, you can use all butter (1 cup of butter instead of ½ cup of butter and ½ cup of lard) with pretty good results.

TIPS

As with any pastry, keeping the ingredients cold will help produce a tender, flaky crust. You can make the pie crust dough ahead of time and keep it in the refrigerator. If you refrigerate it, let it stand at room temperature for 10 minutes or so before rolling it out.

I recommend using a deep-dish pie pan.

FILLING

INGREDIENTS

8 cups apples, peeled and sliced

2 tablespoons lemon juice

3 tablespoons butter

¾ cup sugar

2 tablespoons flour

2 tablespoons cornstarch

1 teaspoon cinnamon

¼ teaspoon salt

¼ teaspoon nutmeg

¼ teaspoon allspice

½ cup apple cider or apple juice

STEPS

- Preheat the oven to 425°F.
- Place the peeled and sliced apples in a big mixing bowl. Toss with the lemon juice.
- In a saucepan over medium heat, melt 3 tablespoons of butter.
- In a bowl, whisk together dry ingredients (sugar, flour, cornstarch, cinnamon, salt nutmeg, allspice) and add them to the saucepan. Add apple cider or juice to the saucepan, whisking to combine.
- Bring the mixture to a simmer, whisking to prevent lumps, and keep simmering and whisking until the mixture thickens (5–7 minutes). When it is thick enough for your liking, pour it over the apples in the big mixing bowl. Toss to coat the apples, then scoop the apples into the bottom pastry crust.
- Roll out the top crust to approximately 11 inches in diameter. Lift the dough as for the bottom crust and lay it over the apples heaped in the deep-dish pie pan. Seal the bottom and top crust together around the circumference of the pie dish however you like – you can tuck the top crust underneath the bottom crust, fold the bottom crust over the top, trim the excess crust and press all along the edge with the tines of a fork, pinch, crimp, or whatever seems best to you.
- Bake for 20 minutes. Reduce the heat to 375° and bake for another 40 minutes.
- Serve warm with sharp cheddar cheese or vanilla ice cream for dessert. Serve leftovers cold for breakfast.

Rosquillas de San Froilán

Makes about 25 rosquillas

GLAZE

INGREDIENTS

1 cup powdered sugar

2 tablespoons water

Splash of vanilla or honey or rum (optional)

STEPS

- Mix the powdered sugar and water in a bowl and set aside. You could also add a little vanilla, honey, or even rum, but try the plain version first.

DOUGH

INGREDIENTS

1⅔ cups milk

1 tablespoon sugar

½ cup butter

1 cup flour

3 eggs

2 cups olive oil for frying

STEPS

- Heat the milk, sugar and butter over medium heat. When all the ingredients have completely melted together and liquefied, add the flour and mix it in with a spatula. Make sure all the flour lumps are gone and the dough has a smooth and consistent texture.
- Remove pan from heat and let it cool down for a few minutes so that the hot dough does not cook the eggs on contact.
- While the dough is cooling, begin heating the olive oil in a large frying pan over medium-high heat. You may substitute canola or other frying oil if necessary, but the rosquillas will not have the same flavor. Olive oil is best.

(continued)

Daniel

Sort of like a cake donut, but a thousand times better. They are eaten in the Spanish region of León on the October 5 feast of San Frolián. Who was San Froilán, you may ask. He was a 9th century monk little-known outside of that area. How long have rosquillas been associated with his feast day? Oh, just a couple of decades.

I surprised you, didn't I? You expected this to be an ancient recipe. Well, the recipe was almost lost to history, it's true, but these rosquillas are a recent invention with an interesting story.

In Spain, there are master pastry chefs – artisanal pastry chefs who specialize in traditional regional pastries, and are as well versed in the history of pastry in a particular region as they are in the art and craft of pastry making. During his mandatory military service, one of these master pastry chefs from León was serving in Asturias, where he hung around and swapped a few techniques with a German master pastry chef who happened to be working there.

When he finished his service, the visiting chef worked in Germany for a while, and then came home to León. He tried selling rosquillas in León, but they didn't catch on. He stopped making them. He liked the recipe, though, so he included it in the textbook he wrote for his culinary school for pastry chefs.

A couple decades go by, and a Spanish master pastry chef from Asturias comes to León and opens a line of fine pastry shops selling Asturian-style pastries ("Confitería Asturias"). Chefs at this level are always keeping up to date on each other's work, so one day he's looking through the recipes in the other chef's textbook and discovers rosquillas. He adds them to the menu, and boom, they're a hit. The feast of San Froilán is suddenly everybody's favorite holiday.

This magical collaboration among German and Spanish chefs would have vanished altogether, if not for the good chef's penchant for constant tinkering – and good record keeping, too!

Be careful: it will ruin regular donuts for you forever. Good food is like that.

STEPS (continued)

- Whisk the eggs in a separate bowl and blend into the dough. The dough will have the consistency of smooth mashed potatoes.
- Prepare a pastry bag with a star tip that will make a tube of dough around ½-inch thick. If you don't have a pastry bag, you can also cut one corner from a plastic food storage bag and squeeze the dough through the cut corner, but you won't get the same nice ridges that the star tip would make.
- Fill the pastry bag with the dough. Lay out parchment paper directly on a cookie sheet or directly on the countertop. With the pastry bag, pipe circles of dough about 2½ inches in diameter onto the parchment paper. It's okay if the end of the circle overlaps the beginning. Leave plenty of space between the circles, because later you will cut the parchment paper so you can put each circle of dough into the oil individually.
- Continue shaping the rosquillas in this way until you have used all the dough.
- When the oil is hot, cut the parchment paper around a few rosquillas and gently lay them, paper and all, on the olive oil, using a skimmer or similar metal tool. The parchment paper will come off as the rosquillas cook. Do not crowd the pan with pastries – this will lower the temperature of the oil too much and they will not cook properly.
- When the rosquillas turn a nice golden brown on the first side, remove the parchment paper as you flip them over to cook on the other side. When the second side has browned, remove the rosquillas from the oil and set them on folded paper towels. Brush them with glaze while they are still hot.
- Serve while they are still warm or when they have cooled to room temperature.

Daniel

Rice pudding is my all-time favorite dessert. Whenever I think of rice pudding, I can smell the milk cooking and the sugar under the flame.

This milk-based dessert is popular in the dairylands of northern Spain, where it is topped with a caramelized sugar crust, a treatment that most people associate with crème brûlée or crema catalana. As far as I know, this way of preparing rice pudding is unique to Spain. The sugar topping is traditionally burned with a hot caramelizing iron, but a brûlée torch produces excellent results and is far easier to use. If you have used a utility lighter to light candles or a barbecue grill, you can use a brûlée torch – just be sure to keep the flame moving back and forth so you burn the sugar evenly. You can also burn the sugar by putting your baking dish or ramekins very close under a broiler set on high. If you go this route, you must be confident that your baking dishes can handle extreme temperature changes without cracking, because they will go straight from the cold refrigerator to a very hot broiler.

Rice Pudding

Makes 6 servings

INGREDIENTS

4 cups whole milk

2 cinnamon sticks

2 fat strips of lemon zest, with the white pith trimmed away

½ cup Arborio rice

1 cup water

1 pinch of salt

¼ teaspoon vanilla

1 tablespoon butter

4 tablespoons sugar

Raw sugar for sugar crust

STEPS

- In a saucepan over low heat, slowly bring milk, cinnamon sticks and lemon zest to a gentle simmer.
- In a separate pot over medium-low heat, combine rice, water, salt and vanilla and simmer. When all the water is gone, stir about 1 cup of the simmering milk into the rice. Let the rice mixture simmer. When it has cooked down a bit and seems substantially thicker, add another cup of hot milk, stir, and let the mixture thicken, repeating this sequence until all the milk (with the cinnamon and zest) is mixed in with the rice. Note: Be careful to make sure milk doesn't stick to the bottom of the pot.
- When most of the liquid has evaporated and the mixture is very creamy, stir in the butter until it is fully incorporated. Remove the pot from the heat. Add sugar and stir until smooth.
- Pour into a single 24-ounce baking dish or 6 individual oven-safe serving bowls or ramekins and refrigerate overnight, or at least a few hours.
- Before serving, sprinkle the surface of the rice pudding evenly with raw sugar or white granulated sugar and caramelize it with a caramelizing iron, brûlée torch, or under the broiler.

TIPS

Many rice pudding recipes call for the pudding to be baked while half submerged in a water bath. I have found that cooking rice pudding like a risotto – repeatedly cooking the mixture down, stirring, and adding more liquid gradually as needed – is faster and prevents the milk from sticking to the bottom of the pot. The taste of burned milk is one of the worst.

If you don't have raw sugar for the sugar crust, regular granulated sugar will also work well.

Carajitos (Hazelnut Macaroons)

Makes 8 macaroons

INGREDIENTS

2 egg whites

Pinch of salt

2/3 cup sugar

1 cup hazelnut flour

STEPS

- Preheat the oven to 350°F.
- Whip egg whites and salt until frothy. Gradually add sugar and continue whipping until the sugar is completely incorporated.
- Fold in hazelnut flour with a rubber spatula. The dough will be soft and sticky.
- With an ice cream scoop, portion dough onto a cookie sheet or jelly roll pan. It is helpful, but not necessary, to line the cookie sheet with parchment paper or a silicone baking mat. Bake for 20 minutes.
- Let the macaroons cool down on the tray for at least 10 minutes before serving.

Daniel

Now I make these cookies any time of the year, but as kids we would enjoy them late in the summer when hazelnut season was in full swing. Hazelnuts are easy to come by in northern Spain, where the trees grow wild on the riverbanks, sometimes as far as the eye can see. The hazelnuts grow in a cluster like chestnuts, but unlike chestnuts' prickly pods, the hazelnut husks are a frilly green that fades and curls back when the nuts are ripe.

These macaroon-style cookies made from hazelnut flour are a traditional late-summer treat in Asturias. The macaroons have a crisp, shiny crust that crackles in baking to show the dense, chewy centers. As delicious as they are, my fondest memories of these cookies are not about their flavor. Instead, they instantly bring to mind the adventures I had climbing thin, flexible hazelnut branches, stretching to the tips of my fingers to harvest one hazelnut after another. Unlike some of my friends, when we were foraging along the river banks I never fell, but I lost plenty of perfectly ripe hazelnuts – plop! – in the water below.

Chris

Ricotta was a staple in my childhood pantry. Mom and Gram used it in fillings for pasta and manicotti, in sweet creams for cannoli and sfingi, as a topping for pizza and even for sandwiches. We always bought our ricotta in 3-pound cans with holes in the sides to let the moisture come out and a pillowy hat of paper on top, secured with a rubber band.

I never even thought about making my own ricotta until many decades later. But the process is so simple and the result so tangy and fresh tasting that it's worth a try.

TIP

Save the whey to use like milk in cakes, cookies, pancakes, etc.

Homemade Ricotta

Makes 2 cups ricotta and 2 cups whey

INGREDIENTS

½ gallon whole milk

Juice of 1 lemon

1 teaspoon salt

STEPS

- Slowly heat the milk to 200°F, just below boiling. Stir in the lemon and salt and let the mixture sit for 10–20 minutes. The milk will separate into curds and whey.
- Line a strainer or colander with 2 layers of cheesecloth. Put the strainer over a bowl or pot to catch the whey and pour the mixture into the strainer.
- Save the whey to use in baking or smoothies.
- Let the curds drain for an hour or so if you want soft ricotta; for drier applications drain overnight in the refrigerator.

Chris

Ricotta with Honey

INGREDIENTS

2 cups whole milk ricotta, drained overnight

1 cup confectioner's sugar

Candied orange peel

Mini chocolate bits (optional)

Honey

STEPS

- Whip the ricotta and confectioner's sugar together until light and fluffy. Stir in the candied orange peel and mini chocolate bits (if desired) and spoon into custard or parfait cups.
- Drizzle with honey and serve with simple butter cookies or biscotti.

Scottish Shortbread

Makes approximately 4 dozen 2-inch-square cookies

INGREDIENTS

1 pound butter

1 cup sugar (plus extra for sprinkling)

6 cups sifted flour

STEPS

- Preheat the oven to 300°F.
- Beat butter and sugar together until very light and fluffy. Add flour gradually, beating well with each addition. Mixture will be crumbly like pie crust.
- Empty mixture out onto a large, rimmed cookie pan, 13x18 inches (half-sheet size), and press flat until smooth. Finish off the top with a rolling pin.
- Use a sharp knife to cut into 2x2-inch squares. Use a ruler. Prick all over with a fork, going all the way through.
- Bake for 30 minutes, then lower temperature to 275° and bake another 30 minutes.
- While still hot, cut along the scored lines and sprinkle with a little sugar. Leave in the pan to cool.
- Store in an airtight tin.

Chris

My wife, Laura, is a nurse. Those of you who are nurses or are married to nurses will know what I mean when I say that it is not a profession but a vocation. Caring and healing are what they do and who they are.

Laura is also an avid tea drinker who derives great pleasure from a steaming cuppa and a simple biscuit. Many years ago, one of her patients shared this recipe for shortbread and it has become one of her favorites. With basically three ingredients – butter, sugar, flour – there is something elemental and magical about the way they combine. It's a perfect example of the kind of transformations that can be achieved by turning simple ingredients into a thing of beauty to enjoy – and share.

Daniel

Technically, clafoutis (kla-FOO-tee) falls into the category of dessert, but at home I regularly serve it as a weekend breakfast. It's full of eggs, milk and fruit, it's easy to whip up in one bowl – and while it bakes you can set the table, make some bacon and coffee and round up the late sleepers. Considering how little effort this dish takes to prepare, the end product looks fairly impressive (especially if you dust it with powdered sugar).

You can use whatever fruit is in season for this recipe, but I prefer plums, cherries or any stone fruit. (The recipe below is for plum clafoutis.) Some say that berries or even grapes work well, and I've used sliced apples with success, but so far plums and cherries remain my favorites.

If you don't have sour cream and buttermilk on hand, you'll get pretty good results with whole milk, half-and-half, plain yogurt, or a combination of those ingredients that adds up to one cup.

Clafoutis

Makes 8 servings

INGREDIENTS

Butter or cooking spray to coat a 9- or 10-inch baking dish

2 cups plums, pitted and halved

½ cup sugar

3 eggs

½ cup olive oil

1 cup flour

½ cup sour cream

½ cup buttermilk

½ teaspoon vanilla

2 teaspoon rum (optional)

STEPS

- Preheat the oven to 400°F.
- Prepare a deep-dish pie plate or other ovenproof baking dish by coating it with butter or cooking spray. Cover the bottom of the dish with pitted plums. (If using cherries, you don't need to cut them in half.)
- In a mixing bowl, whisk sugar and eggs. Add remaining ingredients one at a time, whisking until each is just incorporated: olive oil, flour, sour cream, buttermilk, vanilla, and rum (optional). Pour the batter into the baking dish over the fruit.
- Bake 30–40 minutes, until slightly browned and done to taste. If you enjoy a slightly custardy texture, bake for 30–35 minutes, just until the middle seems set. Otherwise, bake for 35–40 minutes, until batter no longer clings to a cake tester or a toothpick inserted into the center of the clafoutis.
- Serve warm directly from the pie plate, or let it cool before turning it out onto a cake plate. Sift powdered sugar on top if desired. Store in the refrigerator.

Chris

Some years ago I did a cooking show featuring recipes that firefighters cook for their communal meals during long shifts on duty. It turns out that there is quite a tradition of cooking among firefighters and it goes way beyond chili. One of my favorite recipes from that collection was shared by firefighter John Marthens of Engine Company #4 in Pittsburgh. It is a simple scratch cake that turns out fluffy, with a comforting sugary crumble on the top.

Firehouse Coffee Cake

Makes 15 servings

TOPPING

INGREDIENTS

½ cup brown sugar, packed

1 tablespoons cinnamon

2 tablespoons melted butter

⅓–½ cup flour

STEPS

- Mix brown sugar, cinnamon and melted butter. Add enough flour to make a fairly dry crumble. Set aside.

BATTER

INGREDIENTS

½ cup vegetable oil

2 large eggs, beaten

1 cup milk

3 cups all-purpose flour

1½ cups sugar

4 teaspoons baking powder

1 teaspoon salt

STEPS

- Preheat the oven to 375°F.
- Mix first three ingredients together. Add dry ingredients and mix until just combined.
- Pour into a buttered 9x13-inch pan.
- Sprinkle topping over the top of the cake.
- Bake for approximately 30 minutes or until cake springs back when lightly touched.

Acknowledgments

From Chris

Throughout this book you'll read about my amazing mother and grandmother, who taught me the simple connection between food and love.

But I never would have undertaken this project if it had not been for my wife, Laura, who has more faith in me than I deserve and encourages every dream I have.

From Daniel

Thank you to everyone who cooked for me and with me, taught me, tried my cooking, and talked with me about food. Especially...

My abuelita, who wielded her wooden spoon both in love and justice. When she died, I felt like I would never have a home again, but she is with me always in the kitchen.

My daughters, namesakes of their great-grandmothers, who keep trying new foods to please me and discovering favorites to please themselves.

My wife, Laura, who supports and actually finds joy in all my crazy projects.

Our thanks to everyone at St. Lynn's Press for guiding us through this project, and especially our editor, Catherine Dees, who was very gentle with a couple of cookbook novices.

And thanks to the third Laura, our photographer Laura Petrilla, who jumped into this project with both feet even before she knew how deep the pool might be.

About the Authors

DANIEL AGÜERA was born in northern Spain to a restaurant family. He received his formal culinary education in Spain, but his real education as a chef evolved during his travels in Europe, the Mediterranean, the Middle East, and in the U.S., which he calls home. Daniel lives in Pittsburgh with his family and draws inspiration from what is growing at the moment in his abundant kitchen garden. His philosophy is "simple ingredients done well." With *Simple Pleasures,* he shares his favorite home recipes from the Old and New Worlds.

CHRIS FENNIMORE has long been a popular figure on Pittsburgh's WQED public television. Since 1993 he has produced and hosted the series "QED Cooks," winning a James Beard Award and an Emmy along the way. He produced, contributed to and edited more than 100 community cookbooks in WQED's "America's Homecooking Series," used as premiums in membership drives. Needless to say, this lifelong dedicated home cook knows his way around a kitchen. With *Simple Pleasures,* he shares his big Italian-American family's food treasures and memories.

Other books from St. Lynn's Press

www.stlynnspress.com

Dutch Treats
by William Woys Weaver
208 pages • Hardback
ISBN: 978-1943366040

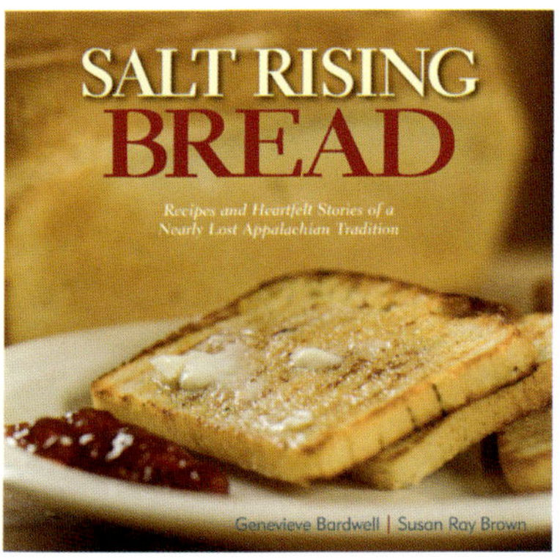

Salt Rising Bread
by Genevieve Bardwell and Susan Ray Brown
160 pages • Hardback
ISBN: 978-1943366033

The Scout's Guide to Wild Edibles
by Mike Krebill
192 pages, Paperback
ISBN: 978-1943366064

The Foodscape Revolution
by Brie Arthur
192 pages • Hardback
ISBN: 978-1943366187